Kaput

Kaput

The End of the German Miracle

Wolfgang Münchau

Swift

SWIFT PRESS

First published in Great Britain by Swift Press 2024

1 3 5 7 9 8 6 4 2

Copyright © Wolfgang Münchau, 2024

Printed and bound in Great Britain by CPI Group (UK) Ltd, Croydon CRO 4YY

A CIP catalogue record for this book is available from the British Library

ISBN: 9781800753433
eISBN: 9781800753440

To Susanne, Joshua and Elias

Contents

Acknowledgements

This book would not have been possible without the generous help of Bill Bollinger, who encouraged me to write it and who agreed to fund the research for it. I am especially indebted to Frederick Thelen, who provided a large volume of research for this book, and whose work informed several of the key chapters in the book – on finance, on Russia and China, on technology and on immigration.

I also would like to thank my colleagues at Eurointelligence, present and past, who have worked on several of the strands in our narrative. Eurointelligence has been an important source for several of the narratives of the book. Anonymous thanks also to the countless colleagues, interlocutors and readers who over the years have contributed to a deeper understanding of the issues I discuss in this book.

Prologue

The town in which I grew up in Germany was not very large, but it had large companies. Mülheim is situated at the western edge of the Ruhr basin, and today has a population of 170,000. On my daily tram journey to my high school in the centre of town, I passed two factories located next to each other. They were surrounded by large grey apartment buildings, characteristic of industrial towns in Germany and other parts of central Europe at the time. The first of the factories made pipelines. The second one made nuclear power reactors. The parents of several of my friends used to work in those factories – some as engineers or managers, and one as a nuclear physicist. Pipelines and nuclear reactors were the gears that powered the German economy. They were the life force of Germany's industrial model.

This was in the 1970s. Back then, Germany was the world's leading producer of nuclear plants, and opted for nuclear power for its future energy needs. Pipelines, too, played an important role in German energy policy, especially after the first oil crisis in 1973. It was these pipelines that would later give Germany access to Norwegian oil and Russian gas.

There was another strand of the German economic miracle that was prominent in the 1970s – that of the self-made entrepreneur. This era of entrepreneurship had started in the late 1940s and early 1950s, and it lasted approximately until German unification. Of all the entrepreneurs in Germany, Mülheim was the home of the country's most successful – and most secretive. Karl Albrecht was the elder of two brothers who, in 1946, took over their mother's grocery store in the neighbouring city of Essen. After the introduction of the Deutschmark in 1948, the two brothers invented a new retail concept – the discount store, with a limited range and very low prices. They called it Aldi, which stood for Albrecht Discount. By 1955, Aldi had already expanded to one hundred stores in the home state of North Rhine-Westphalia. In 1961, the two brothers went their separate ways. The younger brother, Theo, moved to the north of Essen, while Karl moved west to Mülheim, where he ran Aldi Süd.

The Albrechts were the ghosts of our city – ever present with their stores, occasionally spotted, but mostly invisible. We all assumed that Karl lived locally, but nobody really knew for sure. Not only were the Albrecht family invisible to us, they were also invisible to the media and politicians. A local newspaper even went so far as to charter a plane to scour the neighbourhoods where they suspected Karl Albrecht lived, in an effort to find him. The Albrechts never gave interviews. By the time Karl died, at the age of ninety-four, in 2014, he was not only the richest man in Germany, and number twenty in the world, he had also never met a

German chancellor in his lifetime. He, like much of his generation of entrepreneurs, did not owe his success to politics.

The Aldi brothers and the heavy engineering companies I passed on my way to school could not be more different. But, together, they made up the two pillars of the German economic miracle – the corporatist industrial and the entrepreneurial. Aldi is still there, but the entrepreneurialism it used to represent is gone.

The two factories are also still there. Several of Germany's best-known industrial companies were founded in the nineteenth and early twentieth centuries. Some are struggling. Higher energy costs have made industrial companies less competitive. The old Mannesmann pipeline factory is nowadays owned by Europipe, which supplied two of the oil pipelines that connect Germany with Norway. The other company used to be called Kraftwerksunion, a joint venture between Germany's two largest electrics companies, AEG and Siemens. Today, the plant is run by Siemens Energy. The company was briefly in the national news after Vladimir Putin reduced the output of gas through the Nord Stream 1 pipeline during the summer of 2022, a few months after he invaded Ukraine. Germany's chancellor Olaf Scholz paid a visit to the Mülheim plant because he was desperate to get a gas turbine that was sitting there back to Russia so that the pipeline could resume operations. It reads a like a story from a long time ago, but, in the summer of 2022, Germany was still relying on Russian gas. The gas flows ended in late September 2022 with the explosion of the Nord Stream pipelines. The last of Germany's nuclear power stations went offline in April 2023.

The change of my town's fortunes were a microcosm of what happened in the country at large. Germany was the industrial powerhouse of Europe, and the world's largest exporter at one point. But its specialisation created vulnerabilities and dependencies. It became dependent on Russia for gas, and China for exports. Before Brexit, the UK was the largest source of German current account surplus – which measures the gaps between export and imports and investment flows. Then came the break with Russia. Relations with China, the largest trading partner a few years ago, are also no longer what they used to be during the heydays of hyper-globalisation. Perhaps the biggest of all shocks came from technology. Germany was the world champion of the analogue era. But digital technologies have been progressively encroaching into our lives. Germans invented the fuel-driven car engine, the electron microscope and the Bunsen burner. But they did not invent the computer, the smartphone or the electric car. Over the years, that has become a problem.

This book is the story of the rise and decline of a hugely successful industrial giant. It is not a policy book. I am not giving prescriptions for what I feel needs to be done to reverse Germany's industrial decline. That would require a very different and much larger book. This is the story of how and why it happened. Neither is it a 'sick man of Europe' book. The trophy that passes from one European country to another represents little more than a snapshot of the economic cycle. By the time this book is published, I would expect Germany to have come out of the recession that started with the pandemic in 2020 and continued with Russia's invasion of Ukraine in February 2022, lasting until at least late 2023. The underlying malaise, however, will persist, and it is this that forms the subject of this book. The German economic model has come unstuck, and the economic recovery won't fix it.

*

The German social market economy model has a lot of admirers abroad, especially in the UK. One of them, a British journalist and friend of mine, warned me not to write this book. He said the overarching lesson in his professional life had been never to bet against the German economy. What I am trying to do here is to ignore his advice, yet respect the underlying sentiment behind it.

Germany has had its fair share of detractors, who often mock the German obsession with industry and the country's failure to accept that modern Western economies are based on services, not manufacturing. I do share this perspective to some extent. Germans have a far too narrow view of services, which are often seen as an adjunct to industry. But I also feel that the anti-industry sentiment in some parts of the West has gone too far. Industry creates powerful network effects that are often underestimated in places like the UK and the US.

Germany has a history of bouncing back when you least

expect it. Periods of strength were the 1950s and the early 1960s, then from the mid-1980s until the mid-1990s, and again during the first half of the last decade. Could the current weakness that started around 2017 be just another interlude? Would I not be repeating the mistake of so many detractors of the German model if I were to prematurely declare the decline of Germany, only to be surprised later by its rebound?

I think not. Germany's current economic malaise differs in one important respect from those of previous periods. If companies become uncompetitive, the government can cut taxes, introduce labour reforms, or manipulate the exchange rate. But if you are a specialist in making gas heaters or diesel engines, your problem today is not cost, but the product itself. If people are forced to install heat pumps instead of gas heaters, or forced to buy electric cars after the 2035 cut-off for the production of fuel-driven cars in the EU, you have a different problem. While German car makers are still competitive in their classic product range, they cannot compete against the Chinese in electric cars. It's no longer about *how* you do it; it's about *what* you do.

Another important difference is the arrival of new competitors. Germany's reliance on manufacturing exports used to work so well because nobody else did it. For most of the period of hyper-globalisation, from 1990 to about 2020, Germany was unchallenged as an industrial producer. The US, the UK and France had vacated the field. China was not yet there. Since the pandemic, the rest of the world has rediscovered engineering and has started to crowd in on what used to be a German fiefdom. President Joe Biden introduced the Inflation Reduction Act that provided instant subsidies to companies that moved over to the US, in segments like green tech. China, too, shifted its growth model from subsidising infrastructure investment to subsidising manufacturing exports.

The world changed, but Germany did not, and this is a story of how Germany mismanaged industrial capitalism, and misjudged technology and geopolitics. It is also a story of national narratives, the myths we keep telling each other and eventually start to believe. And, like all tragedies, this one begins during the good times.

The post-unification era was the good times. I have a story from that period that gives us an early glimpse of what would go wrong later. By the early 1990s, the telecommunications industry in Germany was still largely unreformed. Deutsche Post, the national postal service, was also the national telephone operator. Using a phone in Germany was a very analogue experience. Whether you had one with an old-fashioned dial or push-buttons, it would take time for the analogue exchange to make the connection. If you are old enough, you will remember the ticking sound – a number nine would be represented by nine ticks. This is why the emergency number in continental Europe is not 999, but 112 – a difference between twenty-seven ticks and four.

By this time, the US had already introduced digital telephone exchanges. One effect was that phone calls were instantly connected. Travelling to the US in the late 1980s, I also noted, to my naïve surprise, that local calls there were free, whereas in Germany you paid twenty-three pfennigs for a local call – and much more for national calls.

In the mid-1990s, as a young foreign correspondent for the *Financial Times* in Germany, I went on a trip with Siemens. It was the beginning of the big telecom liberalisation era. Deutsche Telekom had been split from Deutsche Post and privatised in 1995. It also marked the beginning of a short phase of German shareholder capitalism, similar to what had happened in the UK a decade earlier.

At around that time, demand for mobile telephony services and telecommunication infrastructure expanded rapidly, and Siemens was the main German producer of telecommunications equipment, including the first generation of mobile phones. The phones offered only a few rudimentary services, like text messaging. They were also much larger and heavier than modern smartphones. During the trip, I asked a senior Siemens manager what plans they had for the mobile-phone business. He responded to me, condescendingly: 'You mean, those little devices that people carry?' He left no doubt that this was not a business for grown-ups like him. He then explained to me that the big money was not at the consumer end of the market, but in network technology. Siemens had just produced a state-of-the-art analogue telephone exchange. As it turned out, it was the last of its kind, another piece for the museum. What he did not see was that digital would beat analogue technologies, and that the big money was indeed in smartphones.

Today, it is easy to mock the lack of digital sophistication in Germany – but it is astonishing, if you consider the history. Germany was the country where the digital revolution originated during the twentieth century. German physicists – Max Planck, Max Born, Erwin Schrödinger, Werner Heisenberg – were among those who discovered quantum mechanics, the physics that led to the development of both the nuclear bomb and the semiconductor. Christopher Nolan's film *Oppenheimer* depicts a scene in which the hero as a young man is advised by the Danish physicist Niels Bohr to study in Göttingen. Göttingen was Germany's most famous university at the time and accounted for forty-seven Nobel Prize winners, as well as world-renowned physicists like Born and Heisenberg. Göttingen played an equally important role in mathematics, producing academics such as Carl-Friedrich Gauss, Bernhard Riemann, David Hilbert and Emmy Noether.

All that changed, however, when the Nazis rose to power. Many scientists fled to the US, which at the time had no significant capability in this area. During and after the Second World War, the US became the centre of research into quantum physics, which is the foundation of modern digital technology and digital communications. Its global leadership remains unchallenged, even today. Germany had experienced a similar virtuous circle with the motor car, a product invented by Gottlieb Daimler in the late nineteenth century that kept on giving until deep into the twenty-first century. The big difference is that the era of the fuel-driven car is coming to an end, whereas the digital era has only just begun.

Germany had come out of the Second World War with its great universities depleted of physicists and mathematicians, but it was still hanging on to a few areas of technological excellence, including mechanical and electrical engineering, and chemistry. By the 1970s, Germany was still a player in the early phase of computers and software. (One of the companies founded at the time, SAP, is still a software giant today, the only meaningful German representative in the global tech industry. Of the world's top fifty tech companies, it is the only one that is German. The EU has three, including SAP.)

It was also around this time that the German government started to realise the importance of digital technology. A committee set up by former chancellor Willy Brandt in the early 1970s laid out a timetable for the introduction of optical fibre networks – to get ready for the upcoming computer age. It was a very rare case of German policymakers correctly identifying a mega-trend and trying to plan ahead, and it was probably the best tech call ever made by a German government in modern times. Had Germany stuck by the timetable the scientists suggested, the country would have been years ahead of everyone else in the West in the roll-out of fast digital networks, and the German economy would look very different today.

I remember when my father's company acquired a computer in the mid-to-late 1970s – a monster that took up half the office. The computer was made by Olivetti, in Italy, and ran German software made by SAP. Its software allowed companies to streamline all their invoicing, payroll management, logistics and accounting functions. The personal computer was still a few years away. It was during the 1980s, after the launch of the IBM PC and the original Apple Macintosh computer, that Germany and the other European nations irrevocably started to fall behind the US. But the bigger problem with the Germans was not that they failed to invent the PC, but that they kept betting against the digital universe.

When Helmut Kohl became chancellor in 1982, he favoured schemes that produced gratification in finite political time. Together with the French president, François Mitterrand, he championed high-definition cable television, an analogue-age technology which promised to produce what the two leaders thought would be a massively popular viewing experience. As with many such projects, the implementation took longer than expected and ran into unforeseen technical and regulatory difficulties. In 1990, during the football World Cup in Italy, the Italian state broadcaster RAI transmitted HDTV coverage of the football matches, but it was only shown in eight Italian cinemas. The whole exercise was technically exceedingly difficult, and analogue-era HDTV was formally abandoned in 1993.

In 1995, Nicholas Negroponte, then head of the MIT

Media Lab, published a highly influential book in the US, *Being Digital*. Negroponte explained how digital technologies would encroach into all aspects of our lives – it was not just about desktop computers. He also explained why analogue technologies, like high-definition television or Siemens' analogue telephone switches, were doomed in an age of fast-advancing digital alternatives. Negroponte's book played a huge rule in attuning corporate America and US universities to the opportunities that were lying ahead.

It had much less impact in Europe, except in one unfortunate respect. The digital revolution of the 1990s and the liberalisation of telecommunications in Europe created a short-lived financial bubble, globally known as the dot.com bubble. It was particularly ferocious in Germany, where the dot.com hype was concentrated on a newly created penny stock market, the Neuer Markt. The Neuer Markt saw a flurry of new tech companies being listed, mostly of dubious pedigree, on which many ordinary savers and investors placed large bets. Speculation was fuelled by newspapers and self-declared market gurus, who made their money by providing dodgy share tips. It felt like a modern version of tulip mania, a notorious seventeenth-century bubble in tulips in the Netherlands, the quintessential example of an irrational asset price bubble.

As a member of the team that launched the *Financial Times Deutschland* in 2000, I was living in Hamburg at the time, and I followed the story with increasing exasperation. I remember picking up a taxi from Hamburg's train station late one evening. When the driver found out that I was a financial journalist, he asked me immediately whether I had any special insights into the current initial public offers of a particular company that was about to be listed on the Neuer Markt. He was quite shocked when I told him that I did not know, nor did I care, and that my savings slumbered in a boring investment fund. But I realised at the time that, when taxi drivers ask you about IPOs – in Germany, of all places – things must have gone too far. The market started to collapse a short while later. The Neuer Markt index reached a peak of 9,666 points in March 2000, and fell to 318 by October 2002 – a loss of 96 per cent. That was a crash of tulip-mania proportions – worse, in some respects, as most of the Neuer Markt companies were worthless. If you were unlucky in Amsterdam in 1637, at least you would keep the tulips.

This experience was the German public's initial brush with the digital world. It left Germany with a sentiment of 'never again', as one newspaper put it. In the US, the dot.com bubble also burst, but it was not the end of dot.com, rather the beginning of a new phase of the digital industry, which saw the rise of large digital corporations – Amazon, Apple, Google and Facebook, all American. For Germany, it was the end of dot.com as we knew it.

Germany still had its traditional industries. People do what they are good at, and so, in aggregate, do countries. The US has the digital industry and Hollywood. France has food and fashion. The UK has finance. Germany specialised in cars and mechanical and chemical engineering. By the time of unification, Germany had some of the most illustrious industrial companies in the world, including Siemens, Volkswagen, Mercedes-Benz, BMW, Continental, Hoechst, BASF, Bayer, Linde, Mannesmann and Bosch.

Below those megastars were thousands of medium-sized companies, usually family owned, which tended to operate in niche markets. Many of the so-called *Mittelstand* companies – medium-sized enterprises – were considered the hidden champions of the economy. They were often world leaders in their respective specialisations. In England, the products are often caricatured as widgets – like ball bearings, hydraulic equipment or precision tools, and so many more. But these were hugely successful businesses, and some still are. Many of these companies were world champions of engineering, and had flourished in a post-war Germany that was both entrepreneurial and innovative. The economic miracle was for real.

What happened was that new technology – invented and made by others – intruded. The US economist and journalist Paul Krugman once made a wise observation about trade: the real benefit of trade, he said, comes through imports, not exports. It is hard to imagine a commentary on economics that is more countercultural to the German thinking about economic success than this one. Germans defined success in terms of exports. But Krugman's point is that imports allow you to consume goods and services that you either could not make yourself, or that you could not make at a profit. The same goes for the use digital technologies. You may not be the one who makes it. But you could at least be the one who uses it, or the one who buys a minority stake in the companies that make it. This is what Negroponte tried to tell everybody: digital technologies encroach upon the analogue world. German companies and successive governments did not see that. And when they did, they reached the wrong conclusions and doubled down on what they already had.

A good example of digital encroachment is the modern mobile phone. The smartphone encompasses functions that previously required several mechanical, electrical and other physical devices – the camera, the torch, the compass, the map, the rolodex and, yes, the telephone too – many of which were made in Germany. Smartwatches can already measure our heart rate and produce a long-term electrocardiogram. Digital devices can already, albeit imperfectly, monitor our sleep. In 2024, we are not far away from the introduction of smartwatches that can measure our blood pressure. A smartphone contains sensors but zero mechanical components.

Digital technology is taking over car manufacturing too – Germany's most important industry. A car will always need wheels and axles that turn. But a modern electric car is not a fundamentally mechanical product anymore: most of its value lies in the software and the battery.

As software encroaches on traditional hardware, new companies invariably spring up. The digital giants of today are companies that were founded relatively recently. It was not Smith Corona, the US typewriter company, that invented the PC. Smith Corona tried to integrate the computer into its typewriters and was rather good at it. But it could not think beyond the typewriter. Its strategy worked well, up to the late 1980s – until it didn't.

Germany has a Smith Corona problem. It has been hanging on to old technologies and old companies for too long. Innovation was inextricably linked to existing companies. Innovation was defined by what VW, BMW and Mercedes decide to innovate. That, too, worked until it didn't.

The digital world, by contrast, is a world of start-ups. Start-ups need support – in the form of a strong capital market – and mostly need to be left alone and not encumbered by bureaucracy. Germany offers a great support network for existing companies, but not for start-ups. It lacks a modern venture capital industry. Subsidies are geared towards large companies with legal departments, not to entrepreneurs whose mind is focused on their business. The problem with bureaucracy is that large companies find ways to manage it. Small companies do not.

Since the early 2000s, the gap between Germany and the rest of the world has grown wider. In 2013, Angela Merkel famously called the internet *Neuland*, meaning 'unknown territory'. By that time, the iPhone was already six years old and the US was rolling out Web 3.0. The big-data revolution had started. Germany had already fallen behind in all aspects of digital development, from optical-fibre networks and mobile communications to the roll-out of digital technologies in schools and artificial intelligence. The German healthcare system and police service are still using the fax machine today.

The refusal to adopt modern technologies is, in many ways, the original sin. As time went on, German CEOs and political leaders continued to double down with poor technological, geopolitical and economic bets – and with an economic ideology that equated the economy at large with industry. This is why the biggest concept in the entire German economic debate is competitiveness, something of huge importance for companies, but a concept rarely used for countries. You hardly hear about it in economic debates in the UK or the US. You hear about almost nothing else in Germany.

I recently came across a book written by Hans-Olaf Henkel, a former president of the Federation of German Industry lobby group, who in later life became a member of the European Parliament for the far-right AfD. One of Henkel's big complaints was that Germany had lost the textile industry; he failed to mention that this was the case for every other country in the Western world, too. If he had understood David Ricardo's theory of relative comparative advantage, he would have known that it is perfectly normal for advanced nations to lose certain sectors to developing countries. But Henkel's narrative is the one that stuck in Germany. It is the fight against Ricardo. More competitiveness became the answer to every economic crisis.

In the period from 2005 until about 2015, this focus on competitiveness appeared to work. This is the story of the modern German miracle – the story that got a lot of people confused. Germany managed to prolong an outdated

industrial model for a few more years due to a series of fortuitous accidents. At a superficial level, that decade seems to
be the counter-narrative to my story. At a deeper level, it is
not. That decade is not so much the exception that proves the
rule, but a period that laid the foundations for a future crisis.

The rebound started with Chancellor Gerhard Schröder's
labour-market reforms in 2003. One of the effects was a long
period of wage moderation. The baby boomers were still in
employment at the time, aged between forty and fifty-five.
They had a reasonable standard of living but were fearful
of unemployment. Many would have struggled to find work
elsewhere at that age. The most important was the reduction
in welfare benefits for those who refused to accept job offers.
The reforms and the ensuing wage moderation explain, to
some extent, how German companies managed to improve
their competitiveness against the rest of Europe and the rest
of the world during this period.

At the same time, German industry was helped further by
cheap gas from Russia, the liberalisation of container shipping and logistics, and globalisation that demanded German
plant and machinery. German companies were one of the
main beneficiaries of the global supply-chain revolution.

The fast rise of China and other Asian tiger economies
created a strong demand specifically for industrial plant
and machinery, a technology in which Germany specialises and in which other countries had nothing comparable to
offer. China and India would flood the world markets with
their products. Germany would flood China and India with

German-made production equipment. It was a win–win situation. Until it wasn't.

The euro crisis, which started in 2010, also ended up benefiting German industry in unsuspected ways. The euro crisis was triggered – though not caused – by a massive overshoot of the Greek public-sector deficit at the end of 2010. The crisis spread through the eurozone periphery and, by 2012, it threatened the very existence of the eurozone itself. Mario Draghi, the president of the European Central Bank at the time, intervened and made his famous declaration that he would do whatever it took to save the euro. The crisis caused the massive devaluation of the euro against the dollar, which further raised the competitiveness of German industry by making exports cheaper.

I used to call this a beggar-thy-neighbour strategy: entering a monetary union to fix the exchange rate with your trading partners, and then cut your wages to improve your competitiveness. This, too, worked exceedingly well – until it didn't.

But, for a while, everything had suddenly turned in German industry's favour – the gas, the exchange rate, globalisation and the revolution of global logistics. The fanboys in the national and international media celebrated the new *Wirtschaftswunder*, 'economic miracle'. The trophy of the sick man of Europe had long passed to others.

But it was at this time – the 2010s – when many of the worst decisions were taken. Germany increased its dependence on Russia gas. It underinvested in optical fibre, digital infrastructure and digital technology. It increased its reliance on exports. In the second half of the last decade, Germany registered current-account surpluses of more than 8 per cent of economic output for several years. For an economy the size of Germany, this is unbelievable.

All this is part of what I call the neo-mercantilism mindset. Neo-mercantilism is not a policy. It is a system. And everybody in Germany was supporting it. The main protagonists were the two largest party groups: Merkel's Christian Democrats, the CDU, and her Bavarian sister party, the CSU; and the Social Democrats, the SPD. The Social Democrats have been in government since 1998, with only a four-year interruption. At one level, the goal of neo-mercantilism is to create large export surpluses. It is the twenty-first-century pursuit of eighteenth-century French trade policies, with nineteenth-century companies, using the technologies of the twentieth century. That also worked, until it didn't.

Mercantilists, old and new, are suspicious of disruptive technologies. They like to trade physical goods. The mercantilist mindset goes hand in hand with technophobia. Add the two together, mix in some fiscal and monetary conservatism, a protectionist financial model, and voila, you have the German economic model in a nutshell.

Support for the neo-mercantilist model extends beyond politics, and is also reflected in how the media reports on the economy. Newspapers write about surpluses in the same way they write about football. For several years running, the German media declared Germany the *Export-Weltmeister*, the 'export world champion', despite the fact that this category has no economic meaning. It was a celebration of an economic imbalance – and of a political and economic dependency that later turned out to be very unhealthy, and costly.

The domestic-policy counterpart to neo-mercantilism is corporatism. For a country to pursue mercantilist policies, it needs to work hand in hand with the corporate sector. For decades, governments of the left and right subordinated national politics in the interest of specific champion industries. The CEOs of those chosen industries in turn had special access to government – unlike Karl Albrecht, the entrepreneurial anti-hero of my home town. It felt at times as though the car industry chiefs had their own private keys to the chancellery in Berlin.

This is why errors of judgement in the corporate sector get amplified. Everybody hangs together. Everybody believes in the old industrial model. If you believe, as so many Germans still do today, that you need a fuel-driven-car industry to run a successful economy, you may not spot an electric car when it is coming your way and running you over. The German car-industry chiefs, all male, initially thought of electric cars as toys for girls. VW's erstwhile chairman, Ferdinand Piëch, famously said that there was no space for electric cars in his garage. This attitude was the same as that of the Siemens manager who dismissed the smartphone as a 'little device'. They all committed what I call the Thomas Watson error: Watson was a chairman of IBM in the 1940s who infamously predicted that there would only be demand for five computers in the entire world.

Watson's successors saw it differently, and went on to invent the personal computer. The problem is that, in a mercantilist world, when a misjudgement is made, there is nobody there to correct it. Everybody is in the same boat. The German government colluded with the car industry, and even continued to help them when they installed software cheating devices in order to mislead emissions testers. Instead of investing in software or electric batteries, or investing in companies that made them, the German car industry went to criminal extremes to keep the old technology kicking for a little while longer. What the neo-mercantilists in the German government did was to turn a bad bet by a single industry into a bad bet for the whole country. This was not just a case of beer and sandwiches, as corporatism was known in the UK; it was economics roulette.

I am not making a blanket argument against industrial policy. Industrial policy can be successful – like the US bet on semiconductors in the 1950s, or Europe's creation of Airbus in 1970. What happened in Germany was that industrial policy came at the expense of economic diversification. Germany created a cluster risk by placing a series of correlated bets: they bet on copper cables when the smart money went fibre-optic; Kohl bet on HDTV; Gerhard Schröder's government sold mobile telephone licences in order to maximise government revenue at the expense of network coverage – a problem that persists to this day; Merkel accelerated the withdrawal from nuclear energy and doubled down on her predecessor's energy policies; while to list the policy errors of Olaf Scholz's current government requires an entire chapter of this book. The car industry is a good example of a cluster risk. If it falls, it drags a whole series of other supplier industries with it. In other words, when it rains, it pours. When it stops raining, you will still be drenched.

This is why Germany's economic problems are a 'structural slump', an expression invented by the American economist Edmund Phelps. The structure part in this slump relates to the economic model which Germany has clung on to for far too long. The cycle of good times and bad will repeat, but the structural slump will persist – unless you change the model. And change would have to begin with an economic narrative that is not reduced to competitiveness.

This book tells the story of the fall of neo-mercantilism, and the place to start is with money. The German banking system is the quintessence of German economic exceptionalism. It is in some respects the most extraordinary and surprising part of the story. Much of the rest followed from there.

I

The Canary

Neo-mercantilism is about export surpluses in physical goods. The counterparty is a financial sector that makes this possible: finance and factories are mirror images of each other. The rise and fall of Germany's corporatist financial sector – the ultimate power behind the neo-mercantilist system – foreshadowed the crisis that would later befall the wider German economy.

Germany's banking system consists of three pillars of broadly equal strength – the private banks, the state banks and the mutual banks. This three-pillar structure predates the Federal Republic. The first savings banks were founded in the eighteenth century. Joint stock banks and credit cooperatives date back to around 1850. The modern Landesbanken (state banks) developed from the Girozentralen, banks that transacted payments between the Sparkassen (savings banks). The Girozentralen date back to the early twentieth century.

The state-owned banking system consisted of the KfW Bank – the old bank for post-war reconstruction – the Landesbanken and the Sparkassen. One of the other facts of the German system is that it has underdeveloped capital markets, combined with an overdeveloped state banking sector. This is no accident. For a long time during the first and second phases of the Industrial Revolution, it did not matter much. The banking system was geared towards large and stable corporate environments, and fulfilled many of the functions of an efficient capital market. Banks are not institutions that place bets on unicorns, as is often said of successful starts-up. This is not a criticism of the banks; it is not their job. But a lopsided financial sector makes for a lopsided industrial one.

After the Second World War, the large private banks – Deutsche Bank, Dresdner Bank and Commerzbank – were broken up into regional groups, but were allowed to consolidate again in 1957. More consolidation followed in 2009 when Dresdner was taken over by Commerzbank.

The private banks and the Landesbanken were big rivals. The private banks always complained that the Landesbanken would undermine their profit margins, curtail their growth and stop them from playing in the first league of global banking. But the political establishment across the spectrum supported the Landesbanken over all else because they were ultimately in charge of them.

In the early 1970s, the then German economics minister Karl Schiller discovered a new function for the public-sector banking system: to support the government's macroeconomic policy – for example, its stabilisation policies, through increases or reductions in bank lending in a countercyclical manner. Nobody today would attempt to exert such control over the banks – not so much because the idea is bad, but because politicians no longer have the power to pull this off. But it did work briefly in the 1970s. Of the Landesbanken, WestLB became the most important part of the macro-stabilisation efforts of the government.

Germany's financial sector is not too dissimilar from China's. It is no coincidence that both countries pursue nearly identical neo-mercantilist policies, with the main difference being that central government has a greater role in China, whereas the German system is more decentralised. If you want to understand where power resides in Germany, do not focus only on Berlin: a lot of the important power brokers are in places like Hannover, Düsseldorf or Munich. The German system is one of decentralised planning. (To some extent, that is also true of China, where provincial party chiefs retain powerful positions in their regional economies, but they are not as independent as German state premiers.)

Another feature of the German system is that the Landesbanken were institutions under public law, and thus fully protected from bankruptcy. This created competition issues. The guarantee gave them a better credit rating, which in turn allowed them to offer lower-interest loans. It was not until 2001 that the federal government accepted the

European Commission's request to end the guarantee for all public-sector credit institutions. For some, this moment was the beginning of the end. The guarantees encouraged risk-taking – the wrong type of risk.

The system was run by bankers, but it might as well have been run by politicians. A board at a local Sparkasse would usually be made up of members of the local or district council. A lawyer for the Monopolies Commission gave the example of an engineering company in the North Rhine-Westphalian city of Bielefeld, which got into difficulty and was immediately bailed out by WestLB. WestLB also stepped in to rescue a private TV station, and promoted Cologne as a media centre. When Maxhütte, the Bavarian steel company, got into trouble, a string of publicly owned banking institutions was activated to come to the rescue. Germany fulfilled competition laws in terms of state aid, but most of the actual help was granted through uncompetitive lending practices.

In some cases, the banks were even utilised in election campaigns – for example, in the 1998 election in Lower Saxony, when Gerhard Schröder got Norddeutsche Landesbank to rescue Salzgitter, a steel company. This intervention paved the way to Schröder's election victory that year, and his successful challenge to Helmut Kohl. The Landesbanken are serious political players in Germany. The use of Landesbanken allowed politicians to avoid the usual bureaucratic controls for public investment projects; their lending activities were not subject to parliamentary scrutiny.

Politicians in other countries could only dream of having such funding sources at their disposal. Through industrial holdings, corporate loans, housing construction and numerous investments in regional infrastructure, they were mass manufacturers of pork-barrel spending.

*

In North Rhine-Westphalia, the big power behind the throne was WestLB, the largest of the Landesbanken at the time. In the early 1990s, WestLB organised a hostile takeover in the steel sector. Krupp, based in Essen, in the western part of the Ruhr area, was seeking to take over Hoesch, in Dortmund, some fifty kilometres to the east. In 1991, Krupp had secretly built up its stake in Hoesch shares ahead of the takeover. There was a lot of overlap in their respective businesses.

Friedel Neuber – a Social Democrat known by the nickname 'the Red Godfather' – was the head of WestLB. He was the most influential figure in the corporatist world of North Rhine-Westphalia – the Mecca of heavy industry in Germany. Neuber acted for Krupp. Under his leadership, WestLB secretly bought shares in Hoesch to support the Krupp takeover, and the bank made sure that Krupp ended all of its other banking relationships – leaving WestLB as the Krupp house bank. Then, as *Der Spiegel* reported, Neuber's WestLBbought up shares in Hoesch and then passed his package of shares to Krupp, which then launched his bid for Hoesch.

All this happened with the collusion of the SPD-led government under Johannes Rau, the North Rhine-Westphalia prime minister. By then, Rau had already been prime minister of North Rhine-Westphalia for thirteen years – and he would stay in the job for another seven. A year later, he left to become the German president. Rau was a member of the board of the Krupp Foundation, the owner of Krupp, and has since denied that his government played a role in the takeover or had any decision-making authority. That, too, is a very normal part of the neo-mercantilist system. A lack of transparency and accountability is not a bug, but a feature. Transparency would have killed it.

One aspect of the German corporatist system, as we see in the case with Krupp, is collusion between politicians, bankers and industrialists. The Landesbanken were not just lenders; they took strategic stakes in companies, and were often represented on their boards, alongside supportive politicians. The North Rhine-Westphalia version of neo-mercantilism was particularly fierce. Some called it the Rhine-Ruhr cartel.

While the North Rhine-Westphalians bet the house on steel, the northern Germans went deep into shipbuilding. That, too, turned out to be a very bad idea., because the industry suffered a massive crunch due to global oversupply. Between 2002 and 2013, both Bremer Landesbank and HSH Nordbank became the biggest investors in the shipping industry. By 2013, shipping constituted 20 per cent of Bremer Landesbank's loan portfolio. When the industry hit crisis, the two Landesbanken had to be merged into NordLB. By that time, the decline of the Landesbanken was well under way.

In North Rhine-Westphalia, the cesspit of German corporatism, WestLB played an instrumental role in supporting the clusters of heavy industry in that state. This is how North Rhine-Westphalia ended up with a massive dependence on coal, steel and energy. When we talk about Germany's overdependence on specific industrial sectors, the role of WestLB cannot be overstated.

But, as is characteristic of so many actors in Germany's corporatist world, they, too, were blind to global macroeconomic and geopolitical risks. In 1973, WestLB suffered enormous losses in foreign-exchange transactions in the US. That year, the post-war Bretton Woods system of semi-fixed exchange rates collapsed – foreign-exchange volatility suddenly became an issue after more than two decades of stability. The then SPD finance minister of the state, Hans Wertz, defended those losses as necessary to secure the strong export orientation of the North Rhine-Westphalian economy.

Munich-based Landesbank BayernLB acted differently. Under the influence of the CSU, the bank expanded internationally and invested in the modernisation of the state. This was, in the long run, a more successful strategy, and has enabled Munich to become Germany's high-tech centre. BayernLB was one of the few Landesbanken that knew how to pick at least some winners, including new innovative sectors such as the media, chemicals, energy and electronics. In North Rhine-Westphalia, by contrast, the goal was to save the old structures. But, in both cases, the credit institutions were under heavy political influence. BayernLB's chairmen were high-ranking CSU officials, mostly former state ministers.

WestLB was the quintessential Social Democratic Landesbank. The three men who ran the system there were Neuber, Rau and Heinz Schleußer, the finance minister. They were all Social Democrats. Rau was the big boss, but Neuber was the CEO of the operation. As *Der Spiegel* reports: 'Nothing important would happen without him. He was involved in all the big corporate deals of that era – Thyssen and Krupp, Metro, Gildemeister, Babcock Borsig and LTU. His ambitious tourism plans to forge a tourism group through the former Preussag (now Tui) failed due to the resistance of the anti-trust authorities. Neuber headed numerous supervisory boards at Tui, RWE and Babcock Borsig, among others.'

In the 2000s, the Landesbanken started to expand internationally. Neuber, who was at the helm of WestLB from 1981 until 2001, justified WestLB's international expansion on the grounds that a lot of his midsized clients had become active internationally. But offering international banking services to existing clients was not the main part of WestLB's international activities. They invested heavily in what appeared to be lucrative investments at the time – sub-prime US mortgages. There are no prizes for guessing how that turned out. In the movie *The Big Short* there is a famous scene in which someone makes a reference to stupid bankers in Düsseldorf. These were the guys.

These reckless investments initially looked good on the balance sheet – until they did not. The global financial crisis triggered heavy losses for the Landesbanken. It ended up destroying WestLB, which was finally dissolved in 2012. Without the state guarantee, the bank was not able to absorb the losses. The death of WestLB was not the end of corporatist banking in Germany, but it killed its biggest pillar.

The original goal of the Landesbanken was to provide welfare-oriented financial services and to plug market failures. But mission creep intruded. They abandoned their public-sector functions in the name of globalisation and financialisation. The trouble was that they understood their old business only too well – and not much else. Like the Bourbons, they learnt nothing and forgot nothing. Germany ended up with a toxic banking system.

The North Rhine-Westphalian finance ministry put the total cost of the collapse of WestLB at €18 billion by 2027: €3 billion at the expense of the federal government, €9 billion at the expense of its own state and €6 billion at the expense of the savings banks. Even for a large state like North Rhine-Westphalia, this was a massive hit.

Rainer Kambeck, public finance expert at the RWE Institute for Economic Research, said it was the loss of the state guarantee that did them in: 'The Landesbanken were never in a situation where they had to generate very high returns because they always had the state in the background.

And the abolition of the guarantor's liability has led to fiercer competition. And some Landesbanken have fatally reacted to this by entering into very risky business.'

The Landesbanken were run by the wrong people. The red barons of North Rhine-Westphalian finance were perfectly suited to backroom deals in the steel sector, but they did not understand the functioning of modern financial markets, especially modern financial securitisation structures that did not even exist in Germany. There was nobody who knew what was going on – not in the trading room, not in the executive suite and certainly not on the supervisory board, which was full politicians and trade unionists. Nobody was even able to ask the pertinent questions which a supervisory board member should have been expected to ask. Everybody was incompetent.

One reason for this was the way in which state bankers were recruited. It did not matter what you knew, but whom you knew. During the 1970s, traineeships at the local Sparkasse were highly sought-after. Many school-leavers preferred this route to a university course because it would pave the way for a career in the state banking system. There, a university degree did not matter nearly as much as it did in the private sector. I know a case from my own school where the only available banking apprenticeship place in our town went to the daughter of the local Sparkasse president. Sparkassen were an essential part of the communal infrastructure of German cities, and joining the Sparkasse was a way of entering local politics. If the offspring of the local

Sparkasse president got the one available job, you know what you need to know.

German banking is full of dodgy practices. An altogether different financial scandal took place in Hamburg. Warburg, a local bank, set up a scheme known as cum-ex, which exploited a technical loophole in the German tax system. By buying and selling large volumes of shares before and after the dividend date, they managed to extract large automatic repayments in capital-gains taxes. The damage to state and federal governments ran to over a hundred million euros. It was first described as a practice, but Germany's highest court later declared it a crime.

State-owned banks were also involved in cum-ex transactions – which is astonishing, since they ultimately ended up cheating their owners. HSH Nordbank carried out cum-ex transactions from 2008 to 2011 which deprived the Hamburg treasury of €112 million in tax revenue.

The bank repaid this amount plus interest in 2013 and thus escaped trial in Hamburg, despite overwhelming evidence of serious tax evasion, the facts of which were outlined for the authorities in a detailed report. The mayor of Hamburg at the time was Olaf Scholz. There are still open questions about his involvement in the scandal and the company he kept during those years. Some of the bankers involved were also among the Hamburg SPD's most important financial supporters. Had everybody in the state prosecutor's office and in the Hamburg government done their jobs properly, this would not have happened. HSH Nordbank was sold in

November 2018, for around €1 billion, to a group of investors led by the US hedge fund Cerberus.

Between 2000 and 2012, the total number of Landesbanken decreased from eleven to six. After the HSH Nordbank fiasco, the number is now down to five. BayernLB is still around. But, deprived of the guarantee, they are all a shadow of their former selves.

Crucially, their demise did not reduce the public share in the German banking system: savings banks and cooperative banks gained the market share the Landesbanken lost. The system is less toxic today, because the Sparkassen are not betting on dodgy financial instruments in lands far away, of which they know little. But the fundamental problem of Germany's banking sector still has not been addressed – the German economy remains reluctant to diversify into new sectors, and so it continues to be dependent on industries that are long past their prime.

Germany accounts for 24 per cent of the EU's population and 34 per cent of the bloc's banks. It is not that the rest of the EU has a particularly lean banking system, but rather that Germany is more overbanked than others. And, even in Germany, there were 23 per cent fewer banks in 2021 than ten years earlier. Germany is consolidating, but at a slower pace than others. The wretched WestLB is gone. Others have merged. But the business model continues, albeit with a lot less corrupt energy.

The German financial sector is in trouble. This fact was highlighted in an astonishing report published in 2021 by

Jan Schildbach, an analyst at Deutsche Bank, who committed the ultimate faux pas in German banking: he spoke truth to power. His report had a whistleblower quality to it, something one does not often find in the German corporate sector, let alone in a bank.

Schildbach stated bluntly that the German financial sector was going down the drain. His report criticised BaFin, Germany's financial regulator, over a string of big misses, the most important of which was its failure to spot the Wirecard scandal. Schildbach criticised the three-pillar structure of the German banking sector, saying it was no longer in tune with the times and that it discouraged consolidation. He criticised the 30 per cent corporate tax rate, compared to a 22 per cent global average. Probably the least controversial statement was that Brexit had led to a further fragmentation of European financial markets. He also criticised Germany's failing attempts to introduce capital-backed pensions. The bank ended up distancing itself from one of the most honest reports its analysts have ever produced. Christian Sewing, the Deutsche Bank chairman, was so embarrassed that he felt the need to apologise. In Germany, even the chairmen of private banks act like political players.

The study was later formally retracted, and can no longer even be found on the internet. Speaking truth to power is not something that is generally rewarded in Germany.

It's been downhill since the global financial crisis. The profitability of German banks has declined throughout the last decade – going down 30 per cent – and it remains below the European average.

In 2005, German banks accounted for 11.2 per cent of the cumulative market capitalisation of all companies in the German share index DAX. In 2020, the share was only 1.4 per cent. German banks delivered a total shareholder return of minus 10 per cent over the same period, while the total return of the entire DAX was plus 7.3 per cent.

Deutsche Bank has had very ambitious plans over the years, and some high-flying risk-taking executives, like Josef Ackermann and Anshu Jain. But scandals and poor results from investment banking have ultimately taken their toll. Since the late 2010s, investment banking, once hailed as the business of the future, has been scaled down. Deutsche Bank is now doing what it used to do decades ago – focusing on credit financing in the German market.

The state-owned banks played a huge role in providing long-term finance to Germany's industrial base – companies that would have had difficulty procuring it in the private sector. But, while this is the idealised story, this is not how it worked in practice; rather, the state banks acted as conduits that allowed the federal and state governments to direct funding into the private sector. As one report noted, ownership of banks allowed the government to collect savings and channel it to favoured projects. They became a slush fund to circumvent taxpayers. The large state-owned banks acted as the financial arms of government, crowding out private capital and preventing the establishment of efficient capital markets. On the positive side, they gave some small and medium-sized companies access to capital they would not otherwise have received.

This was a justification that a lot of people, myself included, used to accept. Industries have much longer time horizons than financial investors. The capital markets were not geared towards financing long-term industrial investments, the kind that would only bring benefits after several decades.

The reason I no longer believe this is because industry itself has become very short-termist. The car industry, for example, failed to invest in electric cars early enough, even though the circumstances would have been conducive to long-term investments. The software cheating scandal is the ultimate example of short-termism. I would still characterise the industrial *Mittelstand* – the sector of often highly specialised medium-sized companies – as long-term oriented. They tend to be resilient during recessions, and able to absorb losses because their owners do not need to answer to other shareholders or, especially, financial investors. Germany owes a lot to the state-owned banking sector, but that was before the Landesbanken took on excessive risk.

Another argument in favour of a state banking system is that smaller companies cannot tap capital markets directly, or they may operate in sectors of no interest to venture capitalists. The Sparkassen have been specialising in funding shopping centres, or local business parks. But there is no reason for the state-owned sector to fund such ordinary commercial activity: it is not as though the Sparkassen provide businesses with low interest-rate finance.

The biggest problem, as I see it, is political selection bias. The state banks were ultimately backward-looking, and not geared towards company start-ups. For a long time, Germany had no venture capital industry whatsoever. It does now, but the industry is small in comparison to that of the US. One of the reasons Germany is missing out on high-tech companies is lack of finance. Germany has more than its fair share of talented researchers. But the financial systems cannot support them.

German venture capitalists themselves are not always in the same league as their US counterparts, and tend to focus on classic business ratios, rather than market potential. If this is the focus of conversations between entrepreneurs and the directors of local Sparkassen, it is no wonder a lot of potential start-ups are deprived of funding opportunities. The state banks procured long-term finance only for some companies. They did nothing for others.

Like most things in life, the Landesbanken system did not fail in theory, it failed in practice. The defenders of the system argued that the state served as a hedge against excessive risk-taking by private banks. But it was the Landesbanken that ended up taking the most reckless risks. Whether it was bound to happen is a moot point. It happened. This is how all monopolies fail.

The decline and fall of German neo-mercantilism was foreshadowed by the decline and fall of the Landesbanken.

Twenty years ago, of the top twenty banks worldwide, four were German if measured by asset value, and one – Deutsche Bank – if measured by market capitalisation, Today, they are nowhere in the global rankings. In November 2023, Deutsche Bank was 729th in the global ranking. Commerzbank's ranking was 1,132nd.

German industry and the state-owned financial sector are the twins of the neo-mercantilist system. The difficulties of the German banks foreshadowed the difficulties of German industry by about a decade. Given its roots in the Ruhr area, it would be appropriate to call WestLB the canary in the coal mine.

2

Neuland

The strangest part of our story is how Germany changed from the world's most innovative country to one of its technological laggards. It all started with Johannes Gutenberg's printing press, probably the single most consequential technological innovation of all time, followed by the motor car.

The Second World War, without a doubt, resulted in a decisive break in Germany's scientific and technical capability. Many of the best scientists, like Einstein, left the country. Those who stayed were drafted to work on the Nazi war machine. Some, like the mathematician Felix Hausdorff, committed suicide. The skill set that remained largely intact after the Second World War was engineering. Engineering builds on science, and German engineering built on the sciences that Germans still knew: classical mechanics and chemistry. The US entered a new technological area with the civilian fallout of the nuclear bomb: the invention of the transistor in 1947, the integrated circuit in 1959 and the first desktop calculator in 1967. The rest of that story is only too well known. Today, the US – and, increasingly, China – is running the digital world.

And yet, Germany was successful, during the economic miracle years in the 1950s and 1960s, and then again during the period from 2005 until about 2017. So how can these two stories – of Germany's loss of scientific edge and of Germany's periodic economic success – be reconciled?

Angela Merkel holds a doctorate in physics – but not the part of physics relevant to the digital world. Germany is perhaps the Western country with the greatest alienation from all things digital. It is not just about poor mobile-phone reception. This alienation penetrates all areas of society. Germans are not, in general, technophobes. Germany has its fair share of digital companies. But it is not where the money is – at least, not in Germany.

A frequent guest on German talk shows is one Manfred Spitzer, a professor of neuroscience and psychiatry. He has written books in which he argues that schools should not be using any digital content whatsoever. One of his book titles is *Digital Dementia*. Another translates as *Cyber Sick*. His assertion is that digitalisation is damaging the health of young people, and in some cases proves deadly. He's gone so far as to compare the use of digital content to the consumption of drugs and alcohol. When asked whether children should be taught how to understand modern media, he responded: 'Understand media? We are not teaching our children to understand alcohol, either.'

There are people in the US and the UK who hold similar views. But I cannot think of any who have received the same amount of airtime as Spitzer has in Germany.

His books have sold hundreds of thousands of copies. The lack of nuance is remarkable. This is not about whether children should be using mobile phones. There is a legitimate argument to restrict access to some types of devices and digital content. Rather, Spitzer advocates for a broad cultural rejection of all things digital. It is Germany's version of Project Fear. It closes people off from the possibilities that may stem from digitalisation.

Spitzer is not alone. The German teachers' association also warned against what it called 'forced digitalisation'. Josef Kraus, its president, said in 2015 that there was no evidence whatsoever that children with a computer in school performed better than children without. He said digital devices would deprive children of concentration and perseverance. He is not quite as categorical as Spitzer, but rejected the notion that the digital revolution should have any impact at all on education. In the meantime, schools in other countries have found ways to use digital technologies to their advantage. When the pandemic hit in 2020, most German children had not been taught digital learning, and most German schools had not implemented a remote digital infrastructure. The following comment by Kraus is symptomatic of the digital debate in Germany: 'If you don't know your way around a library, if you don't know your way around an encyclopaedia, if you don't know how to distinguish the important from the unimportant, you won't know your way around the internet'.

This statement is a sign of more than just digital illiteracy. There are ways around the internet that do not exist in the physical world. Children still need to learn how to distinguish the important from the unimportant, but knowledge of a legacy product from the world of Gutenberg is neither necessary nor sufficient for success in our modern world. In fact, Wikipedia is a far superior encyclopaedia than outdated print versions that gather dust on bookshelves. Since most families cannot afford an *Encyclopaedia Britannica* or a German *Brockhaus Enzyklopädie*, technophobia goes hand in hand with elitism. People nowadays have access to information that was never available to them before.

Die Zeit reported that money earmarked for the digitalisation of schools had not been spent. In 2019, the German government and the governments of the federal states decided to invest €5.5 billion into computers in schools. But, to get the money, the schools had to go through a complicated procedure that ended up frustrating the project. The main issue was that schools did not have internet connections, and most of the money was spent connecting them. This was happening in 2019 and 2020. The small city state of Bremen, often derided in Germany as an educational laggard, was the only one to equip all pupils and teachers with tablets. Bremen was the only state that was ready when the lockdown started.

Globally, Germany lags behind in digitalisation generally, and in schools in particular. It is in the lower third of the league table of the Organisation for Economic Co-operation and Development. In 2020, only 33 per cent of German pupils had access to a digital learning platform, whereas the OECD average was 54 per cent.

But these numbers do not tell the whole story, because access to digital devices does not mean that they are used efficiently, or indeed at all. Take the smartboards that are used in German schools as an example – many teachers use them only as digital blackboards. The media researcher Ralf Biermann recorded attitudes among German teachers towards digitalisation and found that teachers, as a profession, are among the first to warn against the negative consequences of digitalisation. I would not be surprised if many of them had read Spitzer.

I do not deny that digital technologies can have negative consequences on children. But, in Germany, the public discourse is focused only on the dangers of digitalisation and not at all on the opportunities. As we will see in this chapter, there is a pattern to this.

The anti-tech trend is also evident in German universities. Thirty years ago, Germany had significantly more students studying a science or engineering subject, or mathematics – the so-called STEM subjects – than the UK. Today, the proportion of STEM students in the UK has surpassed that of Germany. For a country that relies on industry as much as Germany, this is an alarming trend. German schools used to be among the top performers in Europe in the OECD's PISA (Programme for International Student Assessment) studies, especially in mathematics and the sciences. The latest study has Germany occupying a poor twenty-fifth place, behind thirteen EU countries, as well as the UK. As Germany converges to the OECD and EU average, it struggles to maintain a labour market that is heavily reliant on well-trained students in those specific subject areas. Social-science graduates don't end up in engineering jobs.

Germany was still tech-friendly in the 1970s. As we have seen, there were plans to connect every household with a fibre-optic cable by the year 2015. The government did not foresee the internet, of course, but it was clear the world was about to enter the information age and data would need to be transported at high speed. Had this plan been realised, Germany would have had the most modern digital infrastructure of all advanced nations, as opposed to one of the worst.

The big intrusion came in the shape of Helmut Kohl, who was elected chancellor in 1982. Kohl favoured the competing technology of an analogue cable-TV infrastructure for his HDTV pipedreams, which Germany then went on to build in the 1980s and 1990s. Even in the 1990s, in the early days of the internet, the German government continued to double down on copper and coaxial cables, which are much slower than optical fibre when transporting large data over long distances. In 2021, seven out of ten German households were still connected to copper cables, which offer irritatingly slow internet connection speeds.

In 2009, Merkel promised high-speed internet connections

for millions. She said that an internet connection was as important as electricity or water. Her concrete promise was high-speed connections for 75 per cent of households by 2014. By 2020, only 51 per cent of households could achieve internet speeds of fifty megabytes per second, which Merkel set as the definition of high speed. This is no longer the benchmark when 500 mb/s and 1,000 mb/s have become available to consumers. Germany is still lagging behind. The latest data suggest that fibre optic connections only account for 10 per cent of all internet connections. The OECD average is 35.5 per cent. France has 51.4 per cent and Spain a staggering 81.2 per cent.

After the 2021 elections, the three new coalition partners agreed to invest in digital infrastructure. Volker Wissing, the minister heading up the plans, set a target of 50 per cent fibre-optic coverage. But the coalition prioritised other policy areas: money was set aside for an increase in defence spending, the transition to green energy, and and the introduction of a basic citizens' income. The return to the fiscal rules meant there was not much left for investment in digitalisation. More cuts in 2025 are on the way to meet fiscal targets. The biggest saving of all is expected to be in digital infrastructure.

But if there is one thing in Germany that is worse than the fibre-optic cable coverage, it is the mobile-phone networks. Peter Altmaier, the former economics minister, went so far as to tell his office not to route any phone calls to his car because he was embarrassed by the persistent gaps in the mobile coverage. When my family and I visit Germany, someone usually ends up complaining that their phone is broken, when in fact the problem is the absence of a mobile signal. When Germany auctioned off mobile-phone licences, starting in the early 2000s, the priority was not to achieve full coverage, but to maximise revenue. German politicians often defended this decision by arguing that there was no need to connect every remote cow barn. This comment, repeated ad nauseam in debates, betrays a lack of understanding of the nature of digital infrastructure in the twenty-first century. When you cannot get a fibre-optic cable to a remote barn, you absolutely must connect it wirelessly. A mobile-phone network that only works in cities is useless in a decentralised economy.

Lack of public and private-sector investment often go hand in hand. As we have seen, Siemens bet on analogue-age electronics at a time when the digital revolution was well under way in the US. And Deutsche Telekom, the country's main telecoms company, reduced its investments in network infrastructure by 2 per cent each year from 2004 until 2014.

This shortfall in industrial investment has big effects. A 2014 story in *Manager Magazine* reported that a company start-up with sixteen employees had tried to rent office space in Berlin but had faced a six-week delay due to the lack of internet. All mobile providers could only offer slow connections and transitional solutions. There are plenty of stories like this everywhere in Germany. This is the result of chronic underinvestment.

A poor digital infrastructure has had all sorts of knock-on effects. One of the reasons German industry was not able to develop a leading edge in electric cars was its inability to test their connectivity apps, like 3D navigation, on German streets, because of a lack of mobile signal. Even some industrial companies cannot get connected to a fibre-optic cable if they are located too far away from existing infrastructure. I know of companies, and even households, that got together and financed their own private fibre-optic connections.

My favourite story about Germany's slow internet came from the deepest Sauerland, a region of rolling hills and dense forests to the south-east of Dortmund. A photographer needed to send a large photo collection to a printer that was ten kilometres away. The total data volume was 4.5 gigabytes, which is about the size of an average movie. He organised a race – between an internet upload and his horse. He burnt his photos on to a DVD and gave his computer a twenty-minute head start because he had to get the horse ready. The horse not only won the race, but, after riding home and feeding the horse, the photographer found the internet transmission was still uploading.

So why is Germany so behind? Apart from digital illiteracy, another big problem is the coordination between the federal government and the Länder, the sixteen states. The German system of federalism, unfortunately, does not produce clear-cut divisions of competences, but instead there are lots of overlapping areas where both sides are involved. This became lethally obvious both during the pandemic and during the 2022 floods in the Ahr Valley in western Germany. Overlapping competences are also impeding the rollout of digital infrastructure.

Digitalisation has long been on the list of worthwhile government ambitions, but at no point has it been a priority. Successive governments made big promises that remained unfulfilled. In 2018, the federal government promised that Germany would become a world leader in artificial intelligence. Not only has this not happened, but they are not even trying to make it a reality.

The private sector, especially the small and medium-sized company sector, is also under-digitalised.

The big issue for manufacturing is the development of mobile communication. As Germany and the rest of Europe are struggling to roll out their 5G mobile communication infrastructure, China is already planning the transition to 6G, starting in 2025, with a target for a commercial rollout by 2030. The use of 6G will have a direct effect on industry because it allows new methods of production, like smart manufacturing, a technology-driven approach that utilises internet-connected machinery to monitor production.

This foreseeable development will clearly not be mirrored in Germany or anywhere else in Europe. It begs the question: at what point will technophobia impact macroeconomic performance? Maybe this is already a factor in the EU's persistently disappointing economic performance. How long can a modern economy continue to run with such a decrepit digital infrastructure? Will niche strategies in non-digital technologies still be profitable? People will still need precision machine tools, but even in areas where that is the case, like robotics, the added value comes from digital technologies, in particular artificial intelligence. What this means economically is that the niche is becoming more niche.

Small countries often have industries that dominate everything. Large countries are more diversified. The US has a very strong high-tech sector, but it constitutes less than 10 per cent of the entire economy. It is hard to calculate the share of the car industry in German GDP. We know that cars and car components make up some 16 per cent of exports, having peaked at 19 per cent in 2016. My favourite measure is value added – because it disentangles the complex supply chains and isolates those parts of manufacturing activity done in the country. According to Germany's Federal Statistics Office, the German car industry alone constitutes almost 20 per cent of the value added in the entire industrial sector – this is massive for a single industry.

The memorable quote by Charles Wilson, President Eisenhower's defence secretary, comes to mind, here: 'What is good for GM is good for America.' That was the 1950s. Nobody in the US would say that anymore, not even about Google or Apple. But they are still saying the equivalent in Germany. The German version has many names: there is Volkswagen, which also owns Audi and Porsche; Mercedes; and BMW. International car makers also have car plants in Germany: Ford, Opel, and nowadays even Tesla.

Of the forty companies now in the German DAX stock

index, seven are from the car industry. The industry employs 786,000 people directly. Their future is not looking too bright. Many will lose their jobs, especially in supplier industries. The problem is a skills mismatch. A fuel-driven car is a mechanical-engineering product. An electric vehicle is a digital device at heart. Its engine only has a fraction of the parts of a fuel engine – and they are different parts.

The story of how the German car industry fell behind dates to the first decade of the century. Back in 2009, the German government set aside a relatively small sum – €500 million – for the development of next-generation electric cars. But this is not primarily a government failure, since the car industry itself had sufficient resources to make the necessary investments. They started to build electric cars, but treated them as a sideshow. In 2017, Kurt Sigl, the head of the Federal Association eMobility e, told *Augsburger Allgemeine* newspaper, 'The problem is not the subsidy, but the salespeople. Just go into a BMW or VW showroom and ask for an electric car. The answer will be: "Don't do this to yourself. What we have here instead is a special offer of a fuel-driven car with high discounts." This is not something I am just saying. We have tested this. What happened is that the German car industry was asleep at the wheel as the global trend for e-cars took off. When they noticed they had been asleep, they delayed it further.'

Rather than investing into the technology, VW defrauded customers and emissions testers by installing software cheating devices into their engines. The software would detect if a car was undergoing an emissions test, at which point the engine would automatically reduce power and therefore output lower emissions. So, instead of solving the problem of overdependence on a technology that had no future, they doubled down. This behaviour runs through our story like a thread.

The irony is that German car companies were ideally placed to take advantage of the new trends. In the late 1990s, a Daimler-Benz A-class compact car was developed as a potential future electric car – because California had threatened to impose a quota of electric vehicles. When California dropped this threat, Mercedes stopped the development. The A-class had security components that were later used by Tesla. This is another thread that runs through our story. Germany's technological weakness was driven by poor management decisions, and by an excessive sense of the industry's own power. German car companies did not want to develop electric cars because they found them offensive to their own ideas of what constitutes a car.

Another problem was that the German car industry became increasingly short-termist in its perspective. In 2013, Martin Winterkorn, the VW chairman, said VW would build the cars that customers wanted: SUVs. He said electric cars, with a range of 150 kilometres, would not be suitable for long-distance travel. That was indeed a limitation, but clearly that problem would eventually be solved – through better batteries and a better infrastructure of charging stations. The industry either did not see the dynamic or did not want to see it. Winterkorn concluded, back then, that e-mobility would meet its limits.

The German government tragically followed the lead of the car industry. After the diesel scandal broke out in 2015, the transport secretary, Alexander Dobrindt, said he would not be seeking a confrontation with the car companies but instead wanted to cooperate with them. Christian Lindner, the German finance minister and FDP leader, is a very close friend of Oliver Blume, the chief of Porsche and VW. In 2023, the FDP almost managed to derail the EU deal on the 2035 phase-out of the fuel-driven car because Lindner insisted on an exemption for Porsche. The idea was to allow Porsche to produce cars powered by e-fuels. Blume boasted later that Porsche wielded an enormous influence on the coalition agreement. He said that, during the negotiations in Brussels, Lindner had updated him almost hourly. When this story came out, Porsche first denied that Blume had ever said that; when they later acknowledged he did say it, they claimed the quote was meant as an ironic hyperbole. This is the art of the half-hearted denial. What it tells us is that VW and Porsche have the government in their pocket – and that has been the case continuously since Gerhard Schröder took office in 1998.

Schröder was known in the media as the *Autokanzler*. Loosely translated, it means chancellor of, and for, the car industry. It was a car-industry executive, Peter Hartz, who authored Schröder's 2003 economic reform programme. I am not peddling a conspiracy theory when I say that the car industry is running Germany.

There are many problems with corporatist constructs. The biggest one is that when the industry starts to decline, so will the country.

This whole corporatist world lived under the illusion of control – they believed they were in charge and would remain in charge forever. The reality is that, while they were asleep at the wheel in Berlin, Wolfsburg, Stuttgart and Munich, China was busy creating an entire new industry from scratch. The Chinese managed to come from nowhere to become the world's largest car exporter in just a few years. How did they do this?

Government subsidies played a huge role. This could not have been bankrolled by the private sector. But what made it possible was the fact that the e-car is not just based on a different technology, but it is a different product. The Germans produced driving engines, into which they integrated software. They did so with varying degrees of success. The onboard computers of German cars have deep menus with lots of submenus. I was not able to change the time on my German car until I consulted the thick user manual, which told me to find the time function on a third-level submenu in the iDrive section.

Germans were shocked when a Chinese car executive on the TV programme *Auslandsjournal*, in early 2023, spoke only about artificial intelligence, autonomous driving and entertainment systems, as opposed to the qualities normally praised by German car makers, like speed and acceleration. A Tesla is an iPad with wheels – in fact, it's easier to operate than an iPad. You don't need to consult a manual for anything. But the apparent simplicity of the interaction between the human and the car is deceptive. There is nothing more complicated than creating such simplicity, and behind it stands a lot of trial and error – and software development.

What is happening here is not a technical evolution. The electric car works differently and is made by different people. Remember the typewriters? We know how that story ended. Desktop computers and laptops, and the availability of cheap high-quality printers, killed the typewriter industry within a few years. Smartphones, with their sophisticated AI-driven photo software, killed the market for consumer cameras, along with GPS devices, watches, compasses and many more paraphernalia people used to schlep around. When that happens, not only does the product change, but so does the producer. The German car makers are the typewriter champions of our times.

As they used to say in the 1970s: the world will always need typewriters. Until recently, many believed the world would always buy German cars.

The car industry supports a networked supply chain of other interdependent industries. One of the big component suppliers is Continental, a company that, along with many others, has been suffering from the decline in fuel-driven car sales. It has sold 50 per cent of its axle business and is now planning to cut thousands of jobs from its workforce. The company is still selling its braking systems, airbag regulators and displays. But it is making losses.

Germany did not reward those who sought change. In 2022, Herbert Diess, the former CEO of Volkswagen, was fired after the company's supervisory board rejected his ideas for modernisation. He wanted to cut 30,000 jobs in traditional car manufacturing and enhance productivity in the production of e-cars. He also admitted what is generally considered a taboo in the German car industry – that Tesla is technologically way ahead of the Germans in terms of electronic integration. At VW and other large German companies, trade union representatives hold 50 per cent of the seats on the supervisory board. They attacked what they called Diess's erratic eruptions and pushed for his departure. *Handelsblatt* called VW the most change-resistant German car company. It is certainly the most political. And the company is organised like a large bureaucracy. Later, in the same year that Diess left his role as CEO, VW went ahead with job cuts because the manufacturing of electric cars is comparatively simple and requires fewer people. The company's e-cars, however, were flopping in China, where domestic car makers, like BYD, MG and Nio dominate. Tesla continues to sell its cars in the upper e-car segment, where it is the leading producer. The Chinese had increased their market share in Europe from zero to 8 per cent by 2023. The European Commission calculated that this share would go up to 15 per cent by 2025 and has therefore announced protective tariffs of up to 38.1 per cent on imported Chinese electric cars from July 2024.

This is the playbook of how industries decline. After they

have manoeuvred themselves into a corner, they start to call for subsidies and for trade barriers. The consequence will be that EU consumers will pay higher prices for the same product compared to Chinese car buyers. The protected European companies will fall further behind in the technology race, and less money will be available to us for consumption overall.

The Chinese had the advantage of building their industry from scratch. But they did more to create critical mass to harness economies of scale. They invested in the entire supply chain – from the rare-earths elements and magnets, the attempt to corner the global lithium market, all the way up to the car itself. This is what the Germans did so well with the fuel-driven car. They ran a very efficient chain that integrated component supplier, universities and the country's network of applied engineering research institutes.

When the German car makers turned their attentions to e-cars, they encountered problems they did not expect. Most importantly, nobody wants to buy right now – because German e-cars do not offer the same driving experience as a Tesla, and because the German government has failed to invest in a network of charging stations. My contacts in the car industry tell me they don't think Germany will have enough charging stations ready by the 2035 cut-off date for fuel-driven car production. Disappointing sales led to VW reducing the output of its non-selling e-cars at its factory in Emden, north-eastern Germany, through longer holidays and non-renewal of temporary work contracts.

Ford, too, has switched its production in Germany

increasingly towards e-cars, a changeover that also came with job losses. Several thousand Ford jobs are expected to go at the company's technical centre in Cologne, which produces the flagship small car, the Fiesta, due to be phased out soon. As *Automotive News* reported: 'Ford currently employs 6,250 people in product development in Europe. Its next-generation EVs, due after 2030, will use a new, software-defined architecture developed in the US, which means less work for its engineers in Germany.'

Ford is also considering the sale of one its factories in the Saarland region of south-western Germany. Of the 4,500 jobs there, only between 500 and 700 are estimated to remain.

I am not saying that the German car industry will go from a hundred to zero in five years. Germany will still produce cars. But the industry will employ fewer people. And, more importantly, German companies will not dominate the industry as they did in the past. Tesla and the Chinese are the global market leaders. They are also the technology leaders. In China, they control 96.5 per cent of the e-car market. The Europeans are not only considered to be too expensive in China, but they are also seen as antiquated. The software is just not up to scratch.

This is what happens when senior managers focus on how to cheat emissions testers.

At the same time, a large proportion of German car exports go to China, but these are mostly fuel-driven cars. China accounts for 38 per cent of VW sales. Mercedes and BMW sell around a third of their cars to China. But the combined German market share in China has gone down from 25 per cent in 2017 to 17 per cent in 2022. Not a single German car is in the Chinese top ten anymore.

There is an economic expression for the kind of exposure German companies have built up in China: cluster risk. German car companies are heavily dependent on this one country – which is a much more important market to them than Germany itself. Yet they are losing in the fastest-growing market segment. There is still solid demand for expensive German-made fuel-driven cars, especially at the luxury end of the market, so this segment may continue to perform well. But it will not be big enough to sustain the car industry in its current size.

I am reminded of what happened to the manual watch industry after the arrival of digital and smart watches. Rolex is still making money, because the product is not simply a watch, but jewellery. The status-symbol end of the car market may well be the biggest niche for Germany, and a profitable one. But it is small.

One of the strange things that has happened in the car industry, and in other industries too, is that companies have lost their long-term focus. The diesel scandal was a short-term panic response. When I was a young industry journalist in the 1990s, I recall the disdain German managers expressed for Anglo-Saxon financial capitalism and the obsession with quarterly profits. That is perhaps the biggest change in German industry – it is now as short-termist as everybody else.

So why didn't they invest in electric cars ten years earlier?

Or in digital technologies? Or in semiconductors? Wouldn't that have been the long-term thing to do?

When the German government realised that the country's main industry was heading from a massive car crash, they panicked. Their reflex was to focus on what appeared to them the weakest parts of the supply chain: electric batteries. In 2019, Peter Altmaier, Merkel's economics minister, and his French counterpart, Bruno Le Maire, signed a declaration to build a joint battery manufacturer. Two events conspired against the big plans for car-battery production: the rise in energy costs in 2022, and the US administration's Inflation Reduction Act. VW warned that, unless the government started to subsidise electricity costs, it would not be possible to produce batteries.

Shortly after Scholz became Merkel's successor in 2021, he invited the private sector to participate in a discussion on the future of mobility. He only invited representatives of the car industry. Behind this lies the assumption – wrong, in my view – that the next generation of cars will be a continuation of the previous one. I don't think this is what the future of mobility will look like, not even in a car-obsessed Germany. Electric cars are far more flexible. People can use them as normal cars. But, once self-driving cars become a reality, maybe in the next decade, they can be used as taxis and supplement public transport. In the age of the digital car, mobility will mean something very different than it did in the past. Public transport did not feature at all in Scholz's discussions, not even as an afterthought.

The pandemic hit the car industry particularly hard because

of the global shortage of semiconductors. In June 2023, the German government agreed a massive subsidy – €10 billion, a third of the costs for the entire project and historically the largest ever – for a new Intel-chip factory in the east German state of Brandenburg, near Berlin. The goal was to secure chip supplies and to reshore the semiconductor supply chain for the car industry. It was all about the car industry.

The decision has provoked massive criticism from economists, and from those industries who will not benefit from this largesse. Economists have pointed out that the value added from investments into education, research and development would be much higher than from investment in a chip factory in a competitive market. It's also not clear that the factory will increase supply security. As a US company, would Intel not be beholden to its home country? During a state of emergency, would it not be a case of 'America first'? Would Germany be able to stand up for itself when it is so dependent on the US for its security?

Intel is only one of several chip factories that receive subsidies from the government. Infineon is about to invest €5 billion, with €1 billion in subsidies. TSCM of Taiwan, the world's largest chip producer, is planning a €10-billion investment, of which the German government will pay half.

Russia's invasion of Ukraine and the explosions in the Baltic Sea gas pipelines led to an explosion in gas and electricity prices in the summer and autumn of 2022. Energy prices have come down since. But still, the total costs are much higher than they used to be. Without Russian gas, it makes little economic sense to locate high-energy-consuming industries in Germany. The German government pays these massive subsidies because otherwise chip production would not be viable in Europe, but it might have to pay more to keep them alive. This not only carries a cost risk, but a much broader risk of having capital tied up in uncompetitive sectors. Just as they bet the house on the fuel-driven car, they are now betting the house on chips for German-made cars. The German government is doubling down on the car-exports-led growth model. A much better response to a structural energy-price shock would be to allow the economy to diversify into other sectors, and to use government funds to facilitate that transition.

When I speak in Germany to criticise the lack of investment into modern technologies, I usually get looks of utter incomprehension. Germany is widely considered to be one of the world's most innovative countries. The Germans themselves believe this. After all, Germany was ranked as the most innovative country in the world in 2018, in the World Economic Forum's Global Competitiveness Index. How can this be? Is my story all wrong?

It is worth looking into competitiveness rankings in more detail. One important category used to decide a country's place is patents. In the case of Germany, these are mostly old-industry patents. Counting the number of patents and comparing them internationally is a really bad idea, because you are not comparing like with like.

I am not trying to denigrate German technological

innovations. Most of the cutting-edge innovations and patents come in the industrial sector, such as the automotive industry and the chemicals industry. Despite their merits, the innovations that large industrial firms pursue have a lower marginal utility than, say, AI-driven technologies by Google or Microsoft. Innovations in fintech and in other cutting-edge fields, all of which could greatly affect the competitiveness of German industry, are not happening. Germany is relinquishing agency in the global technology race and is focusing instead on the managed decline of the German model.

The German business consultancy Roland Berger published an innovation indicator which was a tad more realistic, but, because of its large-industry focus, still did not capture what was going on under the bonnet. Roland Berger's 2023 innovation indicator has Germany in tenth place globally. In that ranking, Germany is ahead of the US. One should savour this for a second. The US is the leading digital economy in the world. It has the largest tech companies. It is leading in artificial intelligence, robotics and quantum technologies. And it has a blossoming venture-capital market that provides finance for tech start-ups. It is typical of the contempt Germans have for all things digital that innovation in the US is regarded by Roland Berger as too concentrated in just a few sectors. This ignores the fact that these sectors have overtaken classical industry in size, profitability and growth. The Americans also benefit from the winner-takes-all advantage, which is what German industry benefited from in the past. If you are the industry market leader, you reap the highest value added in a global supply chain.

Germany is not doing badly in all high-tech areas – it is still right up there in production technology and energy systems. But it is a global laggard in all things digital.

A very different assessment came in a study by EY, the business consultants, showing that German companies are falling behind in innovation and investments. The big issue is not so much competitiveness, but technology shocks.

VW is a car company at heart that has learnt to integrate software. Tesla started up as a software company and it has learnt how to fit some wheels around a computer. A lot of things that were in the realm of mechanics are these days in the realm of software. Just look at a modern phone. It has various sensors inside, but the value-added high-tech bits are software. The point is not so much that the digital economy is growing faster, but that it usurps some of the old analogue technologies. There will still be demand for German-made precision tools and German-built energy plants. German engineers know how to build nuclear power stations, even if they can no longer use them at home. I am not talking about a binary shift, here. But the growth rates will be lower – and so will the profit margins and the wages. The network effects won't be the same as they used to be.

The very odd thing about Germany's relative digital decline is that some of the country's universities are still right up there, thanks largely to EU-funded programmes like Horizon Europe. The problem is usually the commercial realisation of ideas that come out of academia. In the old world of mechanical engineering, the linkage between German universities and industry worked well. But this integration has failed to be recreated for modern industries.

Krugman's argument, mentioned in the Prologue, that the benefits of trade stem from imports, not exports, can be extended to digital technologies. There is nothing the current or recent generation of Germans could have done to challenge the US as a global tech leader. The USA's position in the industry is closely connected to twentieth-century history and Germany's loss of its leading edge in quantum physics during the Nazi period. After the war, the US was uniquely placed to harness the commercial fruits of what started as a military technology. This produced a technological super-cycle that keeps on giving. The US is still benefiting from the invention of the transistor in 1947. It has maintained that edge ever since, all the way to the latest experimental quantum computers. Similarly, the invention of the motor car guaranteed Germany fat profits over half a century later. The German super-cycle is ending; that of the US is still going strong.

In practice, this need not be as bad it sounds. Even if you are not the main protagonist in the new era, there is still a good second-best strategy: use your accumulated surpluses from the good years to invest in the digital technology, and use the digital technology to improve the productivity of your economy. This is where the Nordic countries are doing so well.

Germany has failed to do either, instead investing its

surpluses into the same old technologies and underinvesting in digitalisation. This is especially true of Germany's *Mittelstand*, the family-owned industrial sector, and the government is not providing incentives for investment in digital technology either. The telecoms infrastructure is often not up to scratch. And there is not enough private-sector capital available for digital projects. Unlike their US counterparts, German venture capitalists are generally not well informed about the latest tech developments.

My views on Germany's flagging ability to innovate are shared by Germany's industrial elites as well. They know, of course, what is going on. Roland Busch, the Siemens chief, told *Handelsblatt* that he sees an acute danger of deindustrialisation in energy-intensive areas like chemicals. He said the regulatory approach to frontier technologies was far too restrictive, and he noted that Germany had essentially already lost the battle for artificial intelligence to the US and China. And he said that his and other companies have huge difficulties getting good people to work for them. Siemens has one advantage over many other German industrial companies: its dependence on China is much lower, accounting for only 13 per cent of its turnover.

Are there perhaps any new champions waiting in the wings? There probably are. Germany clearly missed the digital revolution, both as a supplier and as a consumer, but the country has a lot of tech expertise around, not just in cars and chemicals. Germans are world-class engineers. Our story is not one of inevitable decline. One sector in which

Germany ought to be leading the world is green tech, where Germany's expertise in chemistry, biology and electronic and mechanical engineering all come together. The country is ahead of others in the transition to renewable energies. Is this a potential niche?

The answer is yes, in theory, but the reality is more complicated.

Vertical farming is the practice of growing crops in vertically stacked layers – the agricultural equivalent of urban high-rises, allowing farmers to produce more food on the same amount of land compared with traditional farming. Given the European Union's Green Deal, with its emphasis on nature restoration, one might think vertical farming would be a particularly sought-after technology, but that was not how it seemed to two innovative Dutch farmers when they met the immovable object that is German bureaucracy.

The farmers began their attempts to set up a vertical-farming subsidiary in Germany in 2015, in North Rhine-Westphalia, close to the Dutch border, and were immediately met with opposition from the local council. Initially, there were objections about the number of lorries that would be driving to and from the farm. Then, it was found that the farm they had planned to buy had subterranean structures that needed to be protected. And then there were problems with the extraction of water from the ground, at which point the investors decided to go to Bavaria instead. There, the attempt to set up a farm went well initially, but provoked protests from local vegetable farmers.

Finally, the Dutch farmers found a place where the local, regional and state governments supported the vertical farm – in Brandenburg, near Berlin. Everything seemed perfect: there was enough space, and the place had good connections to roads and electricity. Then, German bureaucracy started to intrude. By now, it was 2020. Five years had already passed since they first decided to expand their business into Germany.

The first complication was a bureaucratic procedure to determine whether the business was agricultural or industrial. The company was classified as agricultural, which meant that a new land-use plan had to be created. A hearing was organised with testimony from forty-two organisations. Agricultural subsidies are capped at €2 million, whereas industrial companies can receive up to 30 per cent of their investment as subsidy. With semiconductor companies it is even 50 per cent – an exception provided for by the EU's Chips Act. But the Dutch farmer got a lot less than the $2 million.

The bigger problem was that this delayed the project further. The delays had cost the investors both time and money – in terms of lost revenues and lost subsidies. They had already bought the site, paying more than €3 million for thirty-six hectares, and had commissioned an energy plan to meet the immense demand with solar and wind energy. Things progressed slowly.

But they did not anticipate having to reckon with the Office for the Protection of Historical Monuments. The civil servants suspected burial grounds from the Bronze Age might be unearthed on the site. This caused further delays, and they were instructed not to dig deeper than ninety centimetres in some places.

Then came another problem. The area allocated to them by the nature conservation authority for cranes was next to a wind farm. The wind-farm operator appealed, citing evidence from another nature conservation authority.

In the meantime, eight years had passed and the market for vertical farming, unfortunately, had changed due to increased energy costs, which altered the investment outlook. At the time of writing, it was still not clear whether the Dutch company would finally get the go-ahead or would sell the land and leave in frustration. The rise in electricity prices would have happened in any case, but they could have had eight years to turn their vertical-farming project into a viable business. It was not a great year to start anything energy intensive in 2023, green tech included. Energy prices started to drop during that year, but, by the spring of 2024, they were still high compared to what they had been before Russia's invasion of Ukraine.

The bureaucratic complications the Dutch investors experienced were not exceptions but features of the system. As a frustrated entrepreneur told *Manager Magazine*: 'Everyone acts according to their rules. Everyone has good intentions, but they only look at their own area. And we seem to fall through all the funding cracks'. This is a good description of what is going on.

This leaves green tech as potentially another lost opportunity. And it got worse with the US Inflation Reduction Act that was specifically targeted at that sector. Unlike EU subsidies, where phantom promises are subject to Kafkaesque bureaucratic procedures, the US is giving real money to companies, immediately, often up front. Many European companies have taken up the offer and left.

Perhaps the most bitter example in Germany is that of Marvel Fusion – a company that is at the cutting edge of research into nuclear fusion technologies. This Munich-based start-up was one of the great German green-tech hopes. But, in August 2023, it decided to move its next big development to the US – to build a new test plant. Marvel Fusion did not get a single offer of investment from Germany or anywhere else in the EU. The money from the US government, of course, was one of the reasons they left. But not the only one. The founder of the company told *Handelsblatt* that another factor was the partnership with the University of Colorado. Such a partnership would not have been possible in Germany, as US universities are more entrepreneurial and partnerships between public institutions and deep-tech companies are better managed.

There was a time, not too long ago, when green tech looked like a plausible new area for growth, even to me. The same was true, many years ago, of artificial intelligence. We think of AI as something relatively new, but research into intelligent systems has been going on for many decades. Algorithms were developed by mathematicians and computer scientists long before we had PCs and mobile phones. In 1991, a German computer scientist at the Technical University of Munich, Jürgen Schmidthuber, and his student, Sepp Hochreiter, managed to overcome a big problem that machine-learning algorithms had faced: the so-called vanishing gradient problem. Their breakthrough gave rise to a special neural network, called the long short-term memory model. It is this technology that stands behind ChatGPT.

You would have thought that Schmidthuber and Hochreiter would be the stars of the German high-tech scene, but, by this stage in our narrative, it's not hard to guess what comes next. Schmidthuber left – not to the US, but to Switzerland, a country that, unlike Germany, has been welcoming to tech start-ups. He founded a company in Lugano to work on commercial applications of AI. He is also the scientific director of the Dalle Molle Institute for Artificial Intelligence Research in the same city.

In 2018, the German government finally published its AI strategy. Like virtually all the initiatives under the Merkel administration, this strategy consisted of bloated claims and poor implementation. The government wanted to set aside €3 billion for research, allocated between various ministries. Much of the strategy was about the role that works councils would play, which tells us a lot about the underlying approach – that existing companies and interest groups would be driving this technology, not the likes of Schmidthuber. It also focused more on the limitations than the opportunities of

AI – which has become typical of the EU approach as well.

It is unsurprising that this initiative did not get anywhere. If there is no single ministry in charge, nothing ever happens. In the medium-term financial planning until 2023, only €1 billion of the €3 billion promised was actually allocated to various ministries.

But this is not the worst of it. The AI plan faced the same problem as Kohl's high-definition TV. It was a bet on the wrong technology. The German government's AI was based on outdated technology, such as expert systems, that was prevalent in the 1980s and 1990s. But the machine learning and deep learning revolution of the last twenty years has completely changed the direction of artificial-intelligence research. It is so ironic that a German computer scientist was at the cutting edge in the early 1990s, and that, thirty years later, the German government is focusing on technologies that were already destined to fail back then. They sought advice from the wrong experts, presumably people who were still conducting research in those areas.

Expert systems use a classic top-down approach. Knowledge is not learnt in these systems, but collected from expert views and stored in large databases. The idea is to funnel tons of information into a system in the hope that something useful will come out of it. Modern neural networks work completely differently. They are modelled on the human brain – highly networked and interactive, and constantly evolving. This is the technology behind the AI in mobile phones, in self-driving cars and in large language models like ChatGPT. Unsurprisingly, expert systems have not really produced any commercial applications.

The issue of the government backing the wrong horse was raised by Florian Gallwitz, a professor of media informatics at the Technical University of Nürnberg in 2019. Helge Braun, Merkel's chief of staff, defended the government's strategy in response to these criticisms, on the grounds that an excessive focus on modern approaches would be too limiting – also in terms of the commercial opportunities. This was another huge commercial misjudgement, but very typical of the way decisions have been made in Germany since the 1980s.

Three years later, Germany and Europe lagged hopelessly behind the US in AI. Germany is way down in the league table of AI start-ups. The US has 5.22 start-ups for each 100,000 inhabitants; the UK has 5.22; France has 2.04 and Germany has 1.9.

Handelsblatt has noted that, of the ten best capitalised AI start-ups, not a single one is in Germany. One of the reasons is that Germany's dedicated start-up centres – in Berlin, for example – are of no interest to the AI industry, which prefers proximity to the top universities. Munich is one of the few such universities in Germany, but is lagging behind the big ones elsewhere in Europe: Oxford, Cambridge, Imperial College London and Paris.

US tech start-ups are benefiting from a community-multiplier effect, being in places where talented people want to work. This is coupled with highly developed venture-capital markets and top universities that specialise in AI, like Stanford, MIT and CalTech.

The European Commission was the first to introduce AI regulation, but the EU is delusional to think of itself as the global regulator for an area in which it has no expertise. It succeeded in other sectors in the past because of the strong presence of European companies. If you don't have any skin in the game, the global regulatory standards will be set by those who do: the US, in this case. Just as Europe and Germany missed out on the first stages of the digital revolution – from the semiconductor to the internet – they are now missing out on the next big stage of artificial intelligence.

It is interesting that, even today, virtually nobody in Germany's political establishment, in any party, is attuned to these issues. The liberal FDP appeared closest when, in 2021, it campaigned on modernisation, including digital investments. But when they came to office, they spent their political capital on fiscal consolidation – as ever, at the expense of public-sector investment. Germany still does not have a digital ministry.

German companies, by and large, are doing better than German politics. Some of them may even build their own niche products based on AI. However, this merely amounts to managed decline, since it is tied to the old industrial model. Medium-sized industrial companies will likely have difficulty adapting to AI, as they cannot draw on the same talent, capital and scale as the big ones. Also, right now, no

German company stands at the forefront of AI development.

The big irony is that Germany has a lot of people working in this area. The number of AI experts, as a proportion of the population, is higher in Europe than it is in the US. It is three times as high as it is in China. The New Responsibility Foundation conducted a study showing that, among the PhD students in artificial intelligence in Germany, 40 per cent were leaving the country. Most of them go to the US, followed by Switzerland and the UK. Of those that stay in Germany, a smaller proportion end up in the private sector compared to PhD students of AI in the US or the UK. The deep problem is not the education and the training of AI experts; Germany is not at the very cutting edge, but it is not doing too badly. The problem is the failure to set up an AI industry. The reason is that neo-mercantilist Germany has narrowed its thinking about economic development to existing industrial sectors only.

In 2020, the outgoing Merkel government started to realise that its approach to the high-tech industry needed a reboot. They created a new federal agency, SPRIND, which stands for Federal Agency for Disruptive Innovation. To me, it sounds like an oxymoron – like civil war or German diplomacy. A German bureaucracy that manages disruption is something to behold. It is modelled on the Defense Advanced Research Projects Agency, better known as DARPA, in the US, which was behind many scientific breakthroughs – for example, the semiconductor and GPS. It's early days. Today, this small and fledgling agency, endowed with an annual budget of only €180 million, is the only part of the federal government with any affinity to the world of high-tech start-ups.

In the public discourse, however, tech start-ups play little or no role. It's all about the old companies. Germany's industrial behemoths have been tremendously successful over many decades. But they owe their success to inventions that happened a long time ago. Still, even in our digital world, we need classical engineering: buses, forklift trucks, cranes and heavy machinery. The brain of a robot is software, but its arms and legs are mechanical devices. But this is no longer a world in which old engineering produces enough money to sustain a trickle-down economic model. The big profits come from technologies in which Germany is not specialising.

Denial, they say, is the first stage of mourning. That phase is still not over. I cannot predict where all this will end, but I can say for sure that the current path is not sustainable. You cannot maintain economic leadership by focusing on economic activities with declining profit margins. Something has to give.

Maybe Germany will adjust eventually. Or maybe German society will accept decline. That would be a decline from a high level. What Germany has not clocked yet is that there is a choice to be made.

3

Low on Energy

The quintessential character of modern German neo-mercantilism is Gerhard Schröder. The quintessential political party of neo-mercantilism is Schröder's SPD. The quintessential industry of German neo-mercantilism is energy. It was none other than Vladimir Putin who brought all of these together.

Around the time of unification – in 1990 – Schröder was the opposition leader in the state parliament of Lower Saxony. He then won an election against Ernst Albrecht, an ally of Helmut Kohl and father of Ursula von der Leyen, who would later become a German defence minister and president of the European Commission.

One of Schröder's early acts was to secure Carl Hahn's successor as chairman of Volkswagen, a company partly owned by the state of Lower Saxony. Schröder ended up promoting Ferdinand Piëch as the new VW boss – a member of the Porsche family and, as it turned out, someone Schröder could do business with. Schröder helped Piëch survive a nasty legal dispute with General Motors after VW hired a senior manager from Opel who had been accused of breaching trade secrets. Piëch and VW were forever in Schröder's pocket.

During his time in Hanover, Schröder surrounded himself with a group of political friends and industry leaders who later become instrumental in the pursuit of his economic policies at a national level. Schröder's most important ally was Frank-Walter Steinmeier, who is Germany's current president. Other well-known politicians were Brigitte Zypries, justice minister and later economics minister, and Sigmar Gabriel, who later became leader of the SPD, as well as economics minister and foreign minister. Another member of the team was the young Lars Klingbeil, the current SPD co-leader. In Germany, political networks such as these carry enormous influence – and they last a lifetime. Olaf Scholz, the current chancellor of Germany, worked as Schröder's general secretary, effectively a deputy party leader, but he was never part of Schröder's inner circle.

The 'friends of Gerhard', as this clique became informally known, had many associate members outside politics. They included Carsten Maschmeyer, the billionaire founder of a company that carries his name, who is married to Veronica Ferres, one of Germany's best-known TV and film stars. Others were Utz Claasen, the former chief of EnBW, the energy company of the state of Baden-Württemberg in south-western Germany, and Peter Hartz, formerly a senior director of Volkswagen, who later became the main author of Schröder's economic reform programme. The list included other energy chiefs, like Michael Frenzel, head of Preussag, and Günter Papenburg, who owned a large construction and waste-management company. All these characters play a role in our story. Papenburg would often travel with then state premier Schröder to Russia to secure lucrative business deals, long before Vladimir Putin entered the political scene in Moscow. This type of relationship became a pattern. It was more than just professional. They all met in a reserved box at the Hanover football stadium and would spend many evenings together at Schröder's house.

Schröder's friendship with Frenzel became critical in the run-up to the 1998 federal election, which Schröder would win against Helmut Kohl. Frenzel wanted to sell Preussag's ailing steel division in Salzgitter, Lower Saxony. The biggest shareholder in Preussag was WestLB, Germany's largest Landesbank, based in Düsseldorf, another SPD-run state. Johannes Rau, the state premier of North Rhine-Westphalia, was a political rival of Schröder. Rau had his own rival circle of friends, the most important of whom was Friedel Neuber, head of WestLB, as I described in Chapter 1. With the help of Frenzel, Schröder managed to push WestLB aside and nationalise the steel business for 1 billion Deutschmarks. The argument was that, otherwise, a foreign company could take over and endanger local jobs. The steel company was renamed Salzgitter AG, after the town where it was located, and later received lucrative orders from Russia.

Salzgitter was only a small piece in Schröder's corporatist

network. The state holding company allowed Schröder's government to interfere in the day-to-day running of Salzgitter and other businesses. It also owned NordLB, the Landesbank, which itself had stakes in many industrial companies. It owned Deutsche Messe, the organiser of the largest industrial trade fair in the world – the Hanover Fair. But the most important stake of all was in Volkswagen, the car giant, which is in Wolfsburg, in the eastern part of the state. As state premier of Lower Saxony, Schröder himself had a seat on the company's supervisory board.

The Salzgitter rescue helped Schröder win the 1998 state elections in Lower Saxony with a near landslide margin, which assured him the chancellor-candidate status of the SPD in the federal elections later that year.

Schröder was the ideal challenger to Kohl. Oscar Lafontaine was chairman of the SPD at the time, and Kohl himself had hoped, and expected, that Lafontaine would be the candidate – a rematch of the 1990 election, which Kohl had won in a landslide. The 1990 election was the first since unification. Kohl embodied the spirit of the united Germany more than any other politician except for Willy Brandt, the elder statesman and former SPD chancellor. Lafontaine represented almost the exact opposite: the radical 1960s generation of the Federal Republic, as Western as it gets. He stemmed from Germany's westernmost state, the Saarland, which is geographically and culturally as distant as it can get in Germany.

But, by 1998, the political fortunes had turned. Kohl had

been in power for sixteen years. First-generation voters had never known a chancellor other than Kohl. Schröder embodied a new start. His corporatism was not the focus of the election campaign. People knew about the Salzgitter stunt, and generally approved of his attempt to save jobs. But he was mostly a reassuring figure. The motto that won him the election was as boring as it could be: 'We will not do everything differently [from Kohl], but many things better'. It represented the public mood at the time. The country had been unified for less than ten years. Globalisation was well under way. Germany was heavily invested in the dot.com bubble that would keep on inflating for another two years before blowing up. Schröder, the manager, seemed to be the right man for the job.

After he came to power, he would pull off another stunt, similar to that of Salzgitter. The following year, he personally intervened to stave off the looming bankruptcy of Holzmann, a large construction company based in Frankfurt. It was a big success. Workers of the company sang chants praising the chancellor. He did not just bang heads together. He used the state-owned KfW bank to provide a €150-million loan and a €100-million loan guarantee that served as an anchor for the financial packages with the various other banks used by the company. The banks would then chip in €200 million. That still was not enough because the company went bankrupt eventually, but it worked for Schröder politically, giving him a reputation for caring about jobs. I saw Schröder as early populist. During the Holzmann crisis, he accused the creditor banks of 'thinking more about their business than securing the company and the jobs' – as though banks would ever do anything else.

A political contemporary of Schröder was Silvio Berlusconi, the Italian prime minister. The two could not stand each other, especially after Berlusconi made fun of Schröder's then four marriages. But the two had something in common: they were the first modern-age populists, centrist and conservative. Both were incredible political campaigners. In 2002, Schröder looked like he would stand no chance against Edmund Stoiber, the CSU chief and Bavarian prime minister. But Schröder managed to beat him hands down because he knew how to run an election campaign.

The Holzmann rescue was dramatic, and characteristic of what was to come. Schröder turned into the most corporatist chancellor of all time. It was in the energy sector that the impact of Schröder was felt the most. Geopolitically, he tried to position Germany between the US and Russia. In that respect, Schröder stood firmly in the political tradition of Brandt and his sidekick Egon Bahr, who was the brain behind Brandt's Ostpolitik in the early 1970s. I met Bahr for an interview in the summer of 1989, and he told me there was zero chance that the two Germanies would ever unify. He was the personification of realpolitik during the Cold War. Bahr was also the architect of Germany's Russia policy at the time. In 1970, the Brandt government signed the first natural-gas contract with the Soviet Union, with pipeline infrastructure supplied by Germany, secured with guarantees from the state-owned insurance company for such large contracts.

'If we connect through a gas pipeline, the political landscape in the Soviet Union will change for the better,' said Otto Wolff von Amerongen, chairman of the German Eastern Business Association. That was one of the most monumental political misjudgements of modern times – one that went unchallenged in German public discourse. And Russia's German friends continued telling each other the same story right up until Putin's invasion of Ukraine. In 2022, the association celebrated its sixtieth anniversary. It was founded in 1952 and sought to foster business relations with the countries of the then Eastern bloc. The German Eastern Business Association is Germany's most powerful lobby, similar to the role played in the US by the National Rifle Association.

The SPD later claimed that its Ostpolitik had contributed to the fall of communism – a claim that plays into German narratives, but is not borne out by facts. Communism collapsed because it failed to provide for its citizens. The collapse was triggered, though not caused by Mikhail Gorbachev's policies of perestroika, which revealed the many deficiencies of the communist system. If anything, Ostpolitik might have contributed to the delay of the breakdown of the system.

Ostpolitik did help German families maintain contact with relatives in East Germany throughout the Cold War, and it reduced barriers, which later facilitated the process of unification. I see this as its most important contribution.

But it also had downright negative consequences. The SPD became blind to human-rights violations in the Soviet Union, and later in Putin's Russia. It was not among the early supporters of Eastern European protest movements, like Lech Wałęsa's Solidarność, which the SPD kept at a cautious distance. I recall an awkward reception in Rau's office in Düsseldorf, which I attended as a journalist, when Wałęsa flew over for a visit. Wałęsa asked Rau for more investment. He was speaking in English. Rau, who was not well versed in that language, appeared to have misunderstood what Wałęsa was saying, believing that he was offering Polish investment in Rau's North Rhine-Westphalia. Rau's relations with other Central and Eastern European politicians were polite, but not close. His relationships with Russian leaders and businessmen were much more personal.

The SPD also had its transatlantic wing. Helmut Schmidt, who succeed Brandt as chancellor in 1974, was one of the most pro-American politicians Germany has ever had, as a result of his close cooperation with the American occupying forces in post-war Germany. In particular, he was one of the few politicians with a deep understanding of US politics. Olaf Scholz, too, is part of the transatlantic wing of German politics.

But Schröder was not. He had a reasonable working relationship with Bill Clinton, as did most European leaders, but not with George W. Bush. After the terrorist attacks on 11 September 2001, Schröder agreed to support the US operations in Afghanistan, an act that cost him a fair chunk of political capital inside his own party. But he broke with Bush and Tony Blair over Iraq, two years later. Vladimir Putin had become his strategic partner in politics, and a friend. I would not characterise Schröder as anti-American. His view was that Germany – as a medium-sized power – should take an equidistant position between the US and Russia. That view was shared by an overwhelming majority of Social Democrats, including Peter Struck, Schröder's formidable defence minister at the time, and Martin Schulz, a former president of the European Parliament who unsuccessfully challenged Angela Merkel in 2017. Until recently, this was a mainstream position in German politics.

Scepticism towards NATO is an outgrowth of this thinking. NATO's spending target of 2 per cent of economic output did not find support in the SPD. Schulz openly rejected it in his 2017 election campaign, where he described it as 'nonsensical and lacking parliamentary legitimacy'.

Schröder's focus during his period as chancellor was to deepen the energy cooperation with Russia. Ruhrgas, the gas company from Essen, was the main actor in this phase of German corporate history. Ruhrgas boss Klaus Liesen sat on the supervisory boards of Volkswagen, the financial-services company Allianz, and Eon, an energy giant created through mergers with the help of Schröder. Liesen was also a member of the supervisory board of Preussag in Lower Saxony. The corporate networks ran deep. The practice of sitting on each other's supervisory boards created an industrial echo chamber, which worsened the already existing bias towards traditional German industries. It was during this time that the digital revolution was really taking off in the US, and the later tech giants were either starting out or, like Apple, heading in new directions. None of that happened in Germany.

Schröder was the godfather of Germany's industrial networks at the time. He soon identified Putin as his most important strategic ally. A personal visit to Putin's house for the Russian Christmas celebrations in early 2001, with the families in tow, marked the beginning of their close personal relationship. In the first two years after taking office, Schröder met with Putin eleven times. The German Eastern Business Association was the biggest cheerleader of that relationship, in support for what it considered Putin's 'wave of modernisation'. It saw an opportunity for Russia to play a big role in the future of German energy policy.

One of Schröder's big domestic projects was the liberalisation of energy policy. It was called liberalisation, but it was not true liberalisation. His government created national champions in the energy market. It was not interested in a level playing field. The government forged the merger of Viag and Veba, both previously state controlled, into Eon. Eon then gobbled up Ruhrgas, the largest German gas company.

The Federal Cartel Office strongly opposed the merger, as it would give the few remaining companies too much market power. Eon appealed to the federal government. First, the independent Monopolies Commission also came out against the merger. Then, the Schröder government overruled both the Monopolies Commission and the Federal Cartel Office, invoking the national interest, and allowed the merger to go ahead. The economics minister at the time, who oversaw this merger, was Werner Müller. The other important player was Alfred Tacke, Müller's deputy, who formally delivered the decision to allow the Eon merger to go ahead. Each of them ended up with a well-paying job in the energy industry after leaving politics. Müller became head of Ruhrkohle, Tacke head of Steag, an electricity provider owned by Ruhrkohle. Readers will not be surprised to learn that Ruhrkohle was also heavily intertwined with Eon.

Schröder narrowly lost the 2005 election against Merkel and retired from active politics. He went on to become the supremo of the Nord Stream company that would build two gas pipelines through the Baltic Sea, connecting Russia with Germany. He knew that German industry needed cheap Russian gas, because it had no alternative energy supplies available.

He also knew that nuclear energy had no future in Germany because his own government had agreed a timetable to phase it out. It was the single biggest policy achievement of the Greens during the 1998–2005 coalition. In 2011, after the Fukushima nuclear accident, Merkel imposed a mandatory nuclear exit by 2023. That decision fortified Germany's reliance on Russian gas. What started as an economic relationship turned into a dependency.

Steinmeier, who had been Schröder's head of the

chancellery, effectively his chief of staff, became foreign minister, and in that role also became Schröder's successor as godfather of German–Russian relations. Steinmeier was fully committed to the idea of modernising Russia through trade, so that it could sustain democratic reforms. As did so many other senior politicians of his generation, he totally misjudged Putin.

Steinmeier suppressed all criticism of Russia within the German foreign office, the government and also at EU level, including during the Russo-Georgian War in 2008. He continued to work closely with industry representatives from Germany and Russia on energy policy to build the Nord Stream pipeline. The first of the two Nord Steam 1 lines was commissioned in 2011, and the second a year later. As Schröder had before him, Steinmeier, too, built up his network of industrialists, putting them in close contact with Russian business partners.

Merkel herself had a more reserved attitude towards Putin. Unlike Schröder, she speaks fluent Russian. I would characterise her as a reluctant follower of the dominant pro-Russia policies that she inherited from her predecessor. She did not dissociate herself from those policies, but the tone was different. The constraints of the neo-mercantilist system prevailed. The mantra of all German foreign policy since the Second World War has been, 'Business first'. Merkel's foreign-policy adviser was Christoph Heusgen, who is nowadays the head of the Munich Security Conference, and her economic-policy adviser was Lars-Hendrik Röller, who was close to the

German Eastern Business Association and a fully paid-up supporter of the business-first approach in German–Russian relations.

The SPD was the party that championed close relations with Russia, but so, eventually, did the CDU and its Bavarian twin, the CSU. After the fall of communism, they no longer saw Russia as an adversary. Here, too, the influence of the German Eastern Business Association made itself felt.

One of the strongest Russia advocates within the CDU was Armin Laschet, prime minister of North Rhine-Westphalia until 2021 and the CDU's unsuccessful candidate in the federal election that year. He was seen as the natural successor to Merkel – and a guarantor of the Berlin–Moscow axis. His state had 1,200 companies that did active business with Russia. His circle of friends was closely involved in leading the German–Russian St Petersburg Dialogue, a Davos-style junket of Russian and German politicians and businesspeople.

The relationship with Russia had become a cross-party project. It was no longer just the SPD. The nexus was industry. Many of the politicians were not necessarily pro-Russian by inclination, but they saw themselves as pro-business and conflated the two. Once the SPD lost power in North Rhine-Westphalia, it was once again the turn of the Lower Saxony SPD to take the lead. Its chief was Stephan Weil, who is the state premier today. He was one of the strongest pro-Russia lobbyists in the party. Being more pro-Russian meant more support from industry, and therefore more chance of winning support from within the party and ultimately winning power.

Connections to the German business elite were also cultivated by successive Russian ambassadors to Berlin. They threw lavish parties at the Russian embassy, attended by the heads of the big automobile, energy and chemical companies, as well as politicians such as Matthias Platzeck, the state premier of Brandenburg and also a former SPD leader, and Schröder himself. Schröder even attended such a party after Russia's invasion of Ukraine.

All this pro-Russian unity lasted until 2015, when Putin annexed Crimea. Merkel responded by organising joint EU sanctions against Russia. For her, this was a game changer, but there was resistance in the grand coalition, both from inside her own party and from large parts of the SPD, including from Steinmeier and Gabriel, and the SPD in Lower Saxony and Brandenburg. Some grandees of the party were also opposed, including Helmut Schmidt and Egon Bahr. Gabriel, who was economics minister at the time, went so far as to oppose the sanctions during a visit to Russia, putting himself in direct opposition to Merkel.

The German Eastern Business Association also pushed hard for the lifting of sanctions, which they saw as a disruptive factor in German–Russian economic relations. Eckhard Cordes, a former Mercedes executive who had become head of the retailer Metro, was its chairman at the time. He repeatedly called for a gradual exit from the sanctions. After Cordes handed over the chairmanship to Wolfgang

Büchele, from the industrial gases company Linde, the position remained the same.

Many in the German business community were direct losers from the sanctions, but the German government, deeply split on the issue, did not supervise compliance with sanctions as much as it should have.

During Gabriel's tenure as economics minister, Germany's dependence on Russian gas grew rapidly: in 2012, the Russian share of gas imports was 34.6 per cent; by 2018, it had gone up to 54.9 per cent, where it remained until 2022, when the Nord Stream pipelines were destroyed.

After the completion of Nord Stream 1 in 2010, Germany and Russia proceeded with the construction of Nord Stream 2, but controversy around the project had grown. Gabriel frequently met with lobbyists, many from the former Schröder entourage. He strongly defended the project, insisting Russia was a reliable partner for gas. Interestingly, the people from Schröder's entourage did not meet with Merkel and her people from the Chancellery, but exclusively with SPD politicians. After Steinmeier became president in 2017, Gabriel succeeded him as foreign minister, a position he held for one year. After the 2017 election, which resulted in an initial stalemate, another grand coalition was formed and the previous justice minister, Heiko Maas, succeeded Gabriel as foreign minister. Maas was not part of the Schröder–Steinmeier–Gabriel Russian fan club, and he was strongly criticised within his own party for his lack of support for Russia, including by members of the executive committee.

The prime ministers of three SPD-led states accused him of damaging German–Russian business relations. The east German states were among the most vehement supporters of relations with Russia, despite the fact that the big industries were mostly located in the west. East German politicians played a leading role in German-Russian diplomacy for historic reasons, one they were reluctant to sacrifice.

At around this time, Merkel started to distance herself, very cautiously, from Nord Stream, and mentioned in her typically understated manner that political factors would have to be considered. Her position brought Germany a small step closer to the EU's much more critical position. The project had provoked massive opposition in Poland and the Baltic states, in particular. A Polish minister compared it to the Molotov–Ribbentrop Pact of 1939 that divided Poland between Communist Russia and Nazi Germany.

The German Eastern Business Association maintained its strong support throughout, arguing that Germany needed the gas. There was no alternative. Scholz took the same position initially, but dropped his support for Nord Stream 2 immediately after Putin invaded Ukraine. Germany's pro-Russian lobby machine, however, continued its support, even weeks after the war began.

The German energy market was firmly in the hands of Russia's majority state-owned energy corporation, Gazprom. In 2015, for example, an asset swap took place with German chemical producer BASF that gave Gazprom control of the largest German gas-storage facility. Gazprom was now not only producer and pipeline operator, but storage owner too. This considerably increased the company's hold on the German energy market, but their prices were cheaper than those of the world market and the deal appeared to provide additional supply security, so it was deemed sufficiently attractive. By the end of the second decade of this century, Germany had become totally dependent on Russia for its gas imports.

Nobody contributed more to making this a reality than Schröder, especially after he left office. He had three bureaus: one in Hannover; one in Zug, Switzerland, where the Swiss holding company of Nord Stream was based; and another in Berlin, where he spent a lot of his time lobbying. He was in many ways still acting in his former role. For example, Schröder took a trip to the Gulf states, where he visited the King of Bahrain with twenty entrepreneurs in tow, just as he had when he was chancellor. Even though he was no longer in office, he continued as the honorary godfather of the neo-mercantilist system, as a door-opener for exporters. He was particularly popular among authoritarian leaders. He said in an interview, in reference to going back to his pre-politics career as a lawyer: 'It was clear to me that I could not use the additional knowledge I had acquired in politics at the district court in Hanover, but rather in the form of consulting at the interface between business and politics.'

In 2007, Schröder helped the Schalke 04 football club get Gazprom sponsorship, which rescued the club from financial difficulties. In 2008, he was guarantor and mediator in the dispute between the automotive parts manufacturer Continental and its major shareholder Schaeffler. At the Swiss publishing house Ringier Verlag, he was employed as a consultant, giving the company access to the Chinese Communist Party. He managed business appointments with Putin and Gazprom boss Alexej Miller. When Eon met resistance in its attempt to take over the Spanish energy supplier Endesa, Schröder was brought in to lobby the case with José Zapatero, the Spanish prime minister and leader of the Spanish Socialists. He even helped the bosses of small businesses – for free – including a producer of underground drilling equipment whom he accompanied through several Chinese provinces. Again and again, Schröder used his influence and access to federal politicians in the service of private companies and industry companions.

A business-first attitude to foreign policy is not particularly unusual. What is strange is that almost nobody in Germany wanted to look too closely at what was happening in Russia. Reports of political assassinations had been circulating in the Western media since the early 2000s. The poisoning of Alexander Litvinenko in London in 2006 was clearly the work of Putin's security services. So was the attempted assassination in 2018 of Sergei Skripal, another former Russian spy, with the Novichok nerve agent. In 2020, Alexei Navalny, the Russian opposition leader, was also poisoned with Novichok, and then, I presume, murdered four years later in a Siberian prison camp. Boris Nemtsov, another Putin critic, was assassinated in Moscow in 2015. Despite all of these and many other political assassinations, the Germans kept on persuading themselves that they could bring about change through trade. That remained their attitude until several months after Putin's invasion of Ukraine.

A typical example of German thinking was revealed in an article jointly written by the late Guido Westerwelle, foreign minister from 2009 until 2013, and Sergei Lavrov, the Russian foreign minister. Appearing in 2010, it called for closer cooperation and a 'modernisation partnership' between Russia and Germany, and, as is often the case in German–Russian relations, referred to the long history between the two countries, harking back to an imperial past and their shared status as great powers that together shaped the European continent. It is unsurprising therefore that this narrative unsettles Germany's Central and Eastern European neighbours, the victims of the power pacts between Prussia or Germany with the Soviet Union or Russia.

This is what the German and Russian foreign ministers wrote: 'This partnership is already bearing its first fruit: in the field of energy relations, which is of enormous importance for the economies of both countries, we have founded the Russian–German Energy Agency, with responsibility for energy efficiency and innovative energy supply. (. . .) And German companies have been involved in Russia for years, while Russian companies are increasingly investing in Germany.'

For the entire period leading up to Russia's invasion of Ukraine, the Germans lived in a state of delusion. The

Russian constitution had forced Putin to hand over power to his prime minister Dmitry Medvedev, and the two switched roles for a four-year interlude from 2008 until 2012. Upon his election, Medvedev announced that he would implement reforms, to the delight of the Germans. They did not see through the Putin–Medvedev deal. The Germans still believed they could democratise Russia. It was unbelievably naïve.

Equally naïve was the idea that interdependence would mitigate geopolitical risk. The federal agency for political education in Germany put out an article in 2006 that revealed an important misunderstanding about political and economic risk. The agency predicted that German natural-gas imports would increase by about 25 per cent, to around 105 billion cubic metres by 2025. Imports from the Netherlands, Denmark and the UK would decline, while purchases from Norway would remain at about the same level. As a result, Germany's imports from Russia would have to increase by about two thirds, to around 60 billion cubic metres. After 2020, they would account for 55 to 60 per cent of total German natural-gas imports.

The article went on to say that this dependence was not a problem because Russia, too, depended on Germany. But what happened is that Germany depended more on Russia for gas than Russia depended on Germany as a customer. There is no such thing in economics as true interdependence. One partner is always in a relatively better position than the other one, whether perceived or real.

Shortly after Putin returned to the presidency in 2012, he gave an interview with the German television broadcaster ARD in which he highlighted the interdependence between the two countries. This was music to the ears of his German interlocutors. In the interview, Putin said:

The structure of trade turnover corresponds not only to Germany's economic opportunities, but also to its interests. For the most important focus of trade and economic relations with Germany is industrial production. I repeat: behind this stand tens of thousands of jobs, incomes of families in Germany and in Russia. Russia covers 40 per cent of Germany's demand for natural gas, and we cover 30 per cent of its demand for oil. We are expanding our cooperation in the high-tech sector, in aircraft construction, in mechanical and plant engineering, in nanotechnologies, in promising developments in the field of physics. This is a very diverse, interesting and promising cooperation. Germany is one of the biggest investors for Russia: there are 25 billion US dollars of accumulated investments in Russia.

Russia's part in this relationship was much more strategic than Germany's. Putin's plan was to build up a Russia–Germany alliance as a counterweight to the US. Russia could not achieve this in partnership with the EU. Putin preferred to work through personal connections, which is more difficult to cultivate in the EU.

German trade with Russia grew constantly until 2015, the year after Russia invaded Crimea. Cars were the biggest exports, followed by plant and machinery – the stuff

Germany does so well. Germany exported engineering gear and imported raw materials from Russia in return. That was the deal. In 2015, there was a sudden downturn in trade due to sanctions – from a total volume of around €70 billion down to around €50 billion. The sanctions affected certain industries more than others. Small-to-medium-sized machinery manufacturers were particularly affected, as the export of machines that could be used for military purposes was banned. Overall, machinery exports to Russia fell by 17 per cent in the second half of 2014. By July 2015, they had fallen by another 30 per cent. Smaller firms in eastern Germany were worst hit, as Russia was often their main market. The sanctions, especially the latest sanctions as a result of Russia's invasion of Ukraine, have played a role in the rise of the far-right AfD in eastern Germany.

Russia's story mirrors that of Germany, in some respects. Both countries have made themselves excessively dependent on just a few sectors – Russia on raw materials, Germany on engineering and chemicals. As a result, neither has felt it necessary to reform the economy. There was no structural modernisation in Russia because Russian elites did not want or need it; they were able to grab the spoils from the resources trade and enrich themselves without investing in modernisation. The division of labour with German companies therefore worked well for them, and it gave them leverage on the international stage. Hence, we can see that initiatives to modernise that might have enabled benefits like visa-free travel were not met. The annexation of Crimea willingly eschewed such potential in favour of a different policy, which was tolerated by German corporate partners.

After Donald Trump was elected US president, he accused Germany of being a prisoner of Russia due to its growing gas dependence and the construction of the Nord Stream pipeline. Due to the anti-Trump mood in Germany, his statement was not taken seriously. But, on this point, Trump was right.

While the sanctions remained in place formally, they were poorly monitored, and companies managed to circumvent them and protect themselves by setting up production facilities within Russia itself – rather than exporting to Russia. This is why German direct investments to Russia skyrocketed in 2015 and 2016. In 2013, investments were at €667 million. In 2014, they slipped into negative territory. But, in 2015, €1.777 billion were invested in Russia, the highest figure since 2010. In 2016, the amount was similar, at €1.075 billion.

For moving production to Russia, German manufacturers received subsidies and other economic support from the Russian state. In those years, German companies became the largest investors in Russia.

BMW wanted to complete a plant in Kaliningrad in 2018 that would handle the complete production of passenger cars. Several hundred million euros were invested in it. Continental built a state-of-the-art tyre plant in Russia, the corporation's most modern and best in the world. The plant opened in 2014 and was taken over by a Russian investment group in 2023. VW also sold a modern manufacturing plant in spring 2023, which had been building 120,000 cars per year for the Russian market for sixteen years before that.

In the weeks after the invasion, the first reaction was one of denial. *Politico* reported that prominent German CEOs in the German Eastern Business Association maintained close ties with Putin and his government through various networks, including the Munich Security Conference. Putin held an annual meeting with important German CEOs at his private residence in Sochi, near the Black Sea. Regular guests were notably Joe Kaeser, an ex-Siemens CEO, and Wolfgang Reitzle, formerly of Linde and BMW.

Kaeser travelled to a business meeting with Putin during the annexation of Crimea, as he did not want to let 'short-term turbulence' affect his business relations, saying, 'It will pass, and we can do business as usual'. A German manufacturer made the confident prediction, after the Western countries imposed sanctions, that the whole issue would be quietly dropped.

In 2022, total German exports to Russia collapsed by 45 per cent. The gas kept on flowing, with the first interruptions happening in the summer. Pro-Russian industry and the trade unions were fighting a heavy rearguard action to maintain the Russian gas supply. They said Russian gas was cheaper and would benefit German industry and workers.

Sections of the IG Metall engineering union criticised American and Eastern Europeans opposition to the Nord Stream on the grounds that they were only pursuing their own interests, selling fracking gas and maximising their profits from gas transit. Trade unions and employers fought on the same side of most battles in that period, including the battle for close German–Russian relations.

Olaf Scholz was outside of that nexus. During the election campaign in the late summer of 2021, he had denied that Germany was dependent on Russian gas. He changed his tune after Russia's invasion the following February. At that point, he argued that Germany could not conceivably be asked to stop the gas flows from Russia because it was dependent on them. The chairman of the German chemicals union also admitted in February 2022 that Germany had no choice but to continue buying gas from Russia. Hardly anybody in Germany ever raised the issue that Germany had become dependent on Russia. Trump did, as we have seen. The German government, meanwhile, actively dissed anybody who spoke out in favour of cutting off Russian gas.

One such person was Benjamin Moll, a German macroeconomist who works at the London School of Economics. After the outbreak of the war, he and his colleagues worked on a paper about Germany's dependence on Russian gas. Their results showed that, while the German economy would go into a recession if all gas imports were stopped, the impacts would not be disastrous.

They were immediately ridiculed, including by Scholz himself, who went on prime-time television to say it was irresponsible to apply mathematical models in a situation like this; he would rather take advice from real businesspeople. Real businesspeople, of course, were parts of the Russia nexus, and they predicted disaster if the gas was cut off. Martin Brudermüller, the head of BASF, asked *Frankfurter Allgemeine*, 'Do we knowingly want to destroy our entire economy?' He predicted the worst recession since the Second World War if Russian gas imports ended.

A consultancy hired by a Bavarian industry lobbying organisation predicted a 12.7 per cent drop in economic output within six months. The German Trade Union Confederation commissioned a study by an economist from the University of Mannheim, who also warned of a drop in output of similar magnitude and a crisis 'the likes of which Germany has never seen before'. The Institute for the German Economy predicted unemployment would rise by 3 million. The chemical lobby initiated a PR campaign, stating that without cheap energy Germany's economy would suffer cardiac arrest.

Moll and his team ran the numbers, comparing a cut-off scenario to a no cut-off baseline. They found that there would be costs to the economy, but that these would be manageable, not apocalyptic. Their prediction was a hit of 0.5 per cent to 3 per cent within a year. Crucially, this figure is less than the recession caused by the COVID-19 pandemic, from which the economy was able to rebound fairly quickly. As it turned out, Moll was right.

This episode clearly shows the influence of industry in shaping the political discourse. From the outside, it could almost appear like the chancellor is doing the bidding of BASF and other industry titans. That has not changed with

Russia's invasion. Scholz is putting the interests of industry first. This is what neo-mercantilism is ultimately about.

This entire debate was brutally cut short on 26 September 2022 when the Nord Stream pipeline suddenly lost pressure – the result, as it turned out, of sabotage. At the time of writing, the perpetrator had not yet been formally identified. Various German news media reported that the investigation of the public prosecutor had focused on a Ukrainian commando. The US journalist Seymour Hersch reported that it was the result of a rogue CIA operation. Others suspected a false-flag attack by the Russians.

Until the Nord Stream sabotage, the gas pipelines had been the one thing that still connected Germany and Russia. With the pipelines no longer operational, the delusions ended.

Psychologists talk about the five phases of mourning, the first of which is denial, followed by anger. The denial phase went on for a long time. The anger was brutal. Anybody with proximity to Putin suddenly fell from grace, no one more so than Schröder himself. Steinmeier was at least as culpable as Schröder, but was spared because he was president and because he was quick to admit he had been wrong. But both Steinmeier and Gabriel have made sure that any official documents relating to their conduct in Russian–German relations will not be released until after 2045. I expect future historians will have a field day with this material, once it comes out. What we have witnessed here is a monumental collective national misjudgement.

This misjudgement had a much larger impact than the size of Russia as a trading partner would suggest. Germany's dependency on Russia for its energy policy had a knock-on effect for the rest of the economy. Schröder's big idea was to generate large industrial export surpluses, for which the country needed a cost-competitive industry. That, in turn, required cheaper and more reliable sources of energy than was available to Germany's competitors. The Russian gas was, in some respects, too good to be true. The catch was the dependency it created.

When the economic strategy of an entire country is framed in such a delusional way, it should not be surprising that further delusions are built on top of existing ones. All the protagonists in our story had a need for Russian gas. Even the Greens party was in favour of gas-powered energy production as it prepared to replace the existing power-supply sources with renewables. Since Germany is neither particularly sunny nor particularly windy, it cannot rely solely on wind and solar for energy production. It needs to have energy sources for when the sky is grey and there is no wind. They chose gas, not nuclear, to solve what is known as the intermittency problem.

The combination of gas and renewables allowed the government to embark on a path to phase out nuclear power. Robert Habeck, the Greens politician serving as economics minister, fought his entire political career for this goal. He was not going to change course just because Putin's invasion unhinged his strategy for renewables, backed up by gas-fired power stations. The Green Party arose out of the anti-nuclear movement in the 1970s; in some respects, the closure of the last three nuclear power plants in April 2023 – two in southern Germany, one in the north – constituted the ultimate victory.

After the explosion of the Nord Stream pipelines in September 2022, Habeck had an excuse to delay the phase-out. But he chose not to. This made Germany more reliant on coal, the dirtiest of all the fossil fuels. Coal is scheduled to be phased out by 2030, but this is not going to be possible now. Over the course of two decades, German energy policy had manoeuvred itself into a dead end. Germany still has access to gas; it built a port terminal for liquified natural gas, or LNG, which it has since procured on spot markets, but at significantly higher prices than the gas from Russia. Prices have been falling in 2023 and early 2024, but the competitive advantage is gone. The only countries with a competitive advantage in energy are those that are relying on nuclear power, those that benefit from fortuitous weather conditions and those that have access to cheap sources of fossil fuel. Germany has none of these.

What strikes me most is the unbelievable recklessness in German energy policy. First, the neo-mercantilists bet the house on Russian gas; then, the Greens bet the house on ending nuclear. When they came to power, nuclear still supplied 14 per cent of German electricity. They had to plug this hole, plus the hole from the loss of Russian gas supplies.

Gerhard Schröder is nowadays a much-diminished figure.

His erstwhile friends in German politics have mostly abandoned him, as has his party, which has even tried to expel him as a member. He is still friends with Putin. A journalist who visited his house in Hanover noted that the pictures on the walls of his office were all of him. There was also a statue – of him. This has a certain Norma Desmond quality to it: I am still big.

Since Putin's invasion, trade with Russia has collapsed and even the German Eastern Business Association is no longer lobbying the government to make up with Putin. It seems the relationship with Russia is over. But not entirely, and not for everybody. Despite the sanctions, there are still many companies doing business with Russia. One was Rheinmetall, the German arms manufacturer, which stopped military exports to Russia after the Crimea annexation but continued to do business in the machinery sector. When confronted about this by a journalist, the company responded: 'There were only isolated activities in the civilian automotive sector and in ground launchers (air-launch units). Deliveries were always made with official approval from the Federal Office of Economics and Export Control.'

Altogether, 70 per cent of the German companies with dealings in Russia before 2022 are still active there. Among them are some of Germany's most influential organisations, such as the Metro Group, Bayer, Bosch, Knauf Gips, Fresenius, Globus and others. In 2022, the Metro Group was one of the top ten companies in Russia in terms of turnover and even expanded its business during the war. This underpins the insistence on business-as-usual and the neo-mercantile model, despite the war and geopolitics. It won't get back to where it was, at least not under Putin or any successor without a broad democratic mandate. That part of German neo-mercantilist history is well and truly over.

But the legacy of that era lives on. Production from energy-intensive industries, such as steel, metal and glass, plummeted after the Nord Stream explosions. It was not until February 2024 that we saw the first signs of a reversal of what had previously been an unprecedented crisis. ThyssenKrupp, the steel company, has cut back 25 per cent of its capacity because it does not expect global demand for its steel to return to previous levels. Its chief executive was seeking an even bigger capacity cut. But many industries that are much less dependent on energy are correspondingly less affected.

Despite this, I feel that too much of the public narrative has focused on energy prices. Energy policy plays a big role in the rise and decline of Germany's industrial model, but the decline is not caused by rising energy prices. The stagnation of German industrial output started well before 2020, and it has only got worse since. The energy crisis is the part that affects old industry disproportionately. Chemical production collapsed in 2023 and BASF has closed several ammonia lines in Germany.

Katarina Reiche, a former CDU MP and now CEO of Westenergie, has noted that the main factor in the increased demand for electricity is new customers like cloud services and internet industries. The latter alone is set to increase electricity demand in Germany by 9 per cent annually.

This is how she believes the situation is evolving: 'In future, the share of renewable energies in the electricity mix is to rise to 80 per cent, so you don't need much imagination to see where the problems arise. There will be change, there will costs, and also stress. We are already seeing an industrial exodus. The energy transition requires implementation-oriented programme management. It does matter where steel is produced or where the chemical industry is at home. We have seen in recent years how fragile value chains are.'

When everything that was considered good one day, is then considered bad the next, we know there is a fundamental problem. It was not too long ago that Germany was widely rated as a stable, well-governed country. The Pew Research Institute noted in 2021 that Merkel's popularity ratings in sixteen advanced economies had reached an all-time high. Public opinion of Germany itself was also positive. Most outsiders held a favourable view of the country and said that it had done a good job dealing with the coronavirus outbreak. But that, as it turned out, was a superficial perspective – as is so often the case with polls.

It only took a few months for the picture to change completely, even though Germany did not change in that period. The close relationship with Russia dated back more than fifty years, but it was during the Merkel years that it turned into a toxic dependency: the unsustainable became unsustained.

Merkel left politics on a high note. But her legacy is in

tatters. Germany is now distrusted by many. Confidence in Germany declined in all NATO countries except the UK and Italy, according to a study by the German Marshall Fund and the Bertelsmann Foundation. Again, one should not make too much of such polls, except to note that views are prone to change quickly.

The big question is whether German politics will continue to do whatever it can to serve the interests of large industry, or whether the country is ready to accept a degree of deindustrialisation and sectoral diversification. Germany will never fully embrace the idea of 'creative destruction', coined by Joseph Schumpeter. The whole German system is geared towards *not* making that necessary. I won't hold my breath here, if only because the decline of industry will not happen in a single big bang but will progress over time. Everybody in Germany is focused on energy and energy prices as the main determinant of Germany's future. They certainly play a role. For steel makers or chemical producers, they constitute the most important input costs. But producing bulk chemicals in Germany really does not make sense any longer. The same goes for several categories of steel.

The far bigger threat to Germany comes from technology, as I explained in the last chapter. But the energy story makes everything so much worse.

4

The China Syndrome

Germany experienced an economic renaissance between 1990 and 2020, but to find out why we need to enter the hard engine room of neo-mercantilism, the industrial workshop, and to look at China's role in the boom.

In the 1970s, German chancellor Willy Brandt was entirely focused on Ostpolitik. He did not follow up on Richard Nixon's visit to China in 1972. For Germany at the time, China was simply not a priority. When I was growing up in Germany during those years, something that was utterly unimportant was referred to as a sack of rice falling over in China. Mercifully, no one would say this today, least of all German businesspeople or politicians. But it took Germany a while to develop a bilateral relationship with China, going from zero to a position of extreme dependence.

When Helmut Schmidt succeeded Brandt in 1974, Ostpolitik continued, but Schmidt was much more global in his outlook. Germany and China had started diplomatic relations in 1972 and Schmidt visited China in 1975, the first German chancellor ever to do so, three years after Nixon's historic visit. Schmidt then did something no German chancellor had ever done: he read up on Chinese culture and history. It was his method of diplomacy – trying to understand his counterparts in their historic, political and economic context. He would not have dreamt of criticising political oppression or human-rights abuses, and in his later years criticised other governments for banging on about human-rights issues. Schmidt would even side with the Chinese leadership after the Tiananmen Square massacre in 1989. Until his death in 2015, he defended what would often be described as a realist position in foreign policy – the acceptance of the world as it was, and the use of foreign policy primarily to improve trade relationships.

Schmidt was not a neo-mercantilist compared with the chancellors that succeeded him. The 1970s were a period with different problems – inflation, global currency instability after the breakdown of Bretton Woods, and, in Germany, the terrorism of the Red Army Faction that culminated in 1977. Schmidt's successors all followed his realist approach to foreign policy. Gerhard Schröder would often call Schmidt to seek advice. The two men had a good relationship.

During that decade, the CDU and CSU were in opposition in Berlin, but nevertheless their state premiers started to forge their own relations in China. The two main parties entered into a diplomatic competition that has continued until very recently. Bavaria, under the leadership of CSU chairman Franz Josef Strauss, effectively developed its own foreign policy in respect of China in the 1980s. The German foreign ministry, run by Hans-Dietrich Genscher, objected to Bavarian grandstanding, to no avail.

Official state visits became more frequent in the 1980s, and Helmut Kohl, who succeed Schmidt in 1982, also received China's leaders in Bonn. Kohl travelled to China with large delegations in 1984 and 1987, and was able to seal the first major joint venture in China after five years of laborious negotiations: Volkswagen was allowed to build a plant in Shanghai, to produce a saloon car under the Santana brand. It was an early foothold in what would become VW's biggest market.

It was also the starting point of the business-first approach to German foreign policy that persisted until the elections of 2021. It was the start of neo-mercantilism.

The Tiananmen Square massacre in 1989 marked the beginning of a change in Western attitudes towards China. But German governments were largely immune to the outrage. Nonetheless, Schmidt's pro-China position did not appear to prevail. The Bundestag, like other parliaments, imposed economic sanctions against China in 1990. The most painful measure was the removal of export credit guarantees, granted by the German government to companies through an insurance service, which in Germany goes by the name of Hermes. This state credit guarantee constitutes an important instrument in the financial toolkit of the neo-mercantilist model. The German government essentially funded the country's risk to allow companies to focus entirely on business. This type of insurance has its downsides, because it encourages apolitical thinking among companies – something that has turned into a big problem in more recent years.

In June 1990, Kohl and Genscher demanded from their own parliamentary groups that they reopen the export insurance guarantees. They MPs did so in October that year, and one of the first projects Germany helped build was the Shanghai metro. China quickly became, once again, the largest recipient of German development aid. Tiananmen Square had been largely forgotten. In the end, Schmidt's position did prevail, after all.

Something else happened in the 1990s that would become critical. Toyota invented a whole new way of managing complex supply chains through just-in-time production. It was a giant optimisation exercise, designed to create the most efficient flow of goods, with minimal storage, minimising idle time for workers. The cliché was for a lorry to offload directly on to a conveyor belt. The idea was first described in the 1990 book, *The Machine that Changed the World*.

It did not quite have the news impact of the launch of the first PC in the 1980s, or the iPhone in 2007, but, for manufacturing, this was a comparatively important innovation. The new method changed German manufacturing like nothing had since the invention of the steam engine and the availability of national and international transport networks. For three decades, industry managed to extract the benefits of just-in-time production. It was a productivity miracle machine that slashed warehousing costs, which would otherwise take up a considerable portion of turnover. We are talking double-digit percentages, here.

It also changed the relationship between a large industrial company and its, usually, smaller suppliers. 'Outsourcing production to a supplier creates a mutual dependency, but there are also advantages for both partners,' writes Jens Südekum and co-authors. 'Larger volumes and longer-term capacity utilisation allow the subcontracting company to realise cost-cutting and the buyer gets almost inventory-free manufacturing in a few strategically important production locations.'

The process created winners and losers, but on aggregate it created more winners. At least, it did in the beginning. There are parallels to the gains and losses from trade: when countries open to trade for the first time, they achieve the large benefits that trade theories of earlier generations predicted. Problems arise later, when the benefits of further trade integration become more marginal, and the cost of compensating the losers rises disproportionately. Just-in-time supply chains would later meet their nemesis during the pandemic, but, back in the 1990s, it was early days – the good days.

The opening up of China and the new production technology produced a whole new dimension to German investment in China. The great age of outsourcing was about to start – 'offshoring', as the Americans called it.

Unlike the US, however, the German experience with offshoring was mostly positive. Germany did not lose companies to

China in that period but managed to integrate China and other Asian countries into their own supply chains. Back in those days, Germany was clearly the senior partner in the relationship. In the 1990s, the composition of supply chains, especially in the car industry, changed. Manufacturers, inspired by the Toyota model and lean production, restructured in favour of outsourcing and just-in-time delivery to reduce inventory costs.

The traditional heavyweights of German industry in particular benefited from the new just-in-time doctrine. The winners were the industrial mechanical-engineering companies, the car makers, steel and metal producers and the chemical industry. The losers were textile, clothing and leather, and the food industries. It was interesting that the winners all used the new Toyota model, whereas the losers were still stockpiling.

The 1990s were an era of Western exuberance. The West had won the Cold War, and the rest of the world had integrated politically and economically with the West. After the conservative 1980s, the centre-left returned to power: Bill Clinton in 1993, Tony Blair in 1997 and Schröder in 1998. It was a decade of big trade deals, like the North Atlantic Free Trade Agreement between the US, Canada and Mexico. It marked the beginning of the World Trade Organisation. The wealth of the decade was amplified by a series of financial bubbles and crashes – the US bond market in 1994, the Asian and Russian financial crises of the late 1990s, the demise of Long-Term Capital Management in 1998 and the subsequent dot.com bubble, which blew up in early 2000.

The prosperity of that period also gave rise to serious misjudgements about globalisation. Western countries, Germany included, mistakenly believed that China, like Eastern Europe, wanted nothing more than to turn itself into a Western-style democracy. The West had, and still has today, a predominant belief that everybody wants to be like us and live by our standards. It was true for Central and Eastern Europe because these countries were communist not by choice but by force. The Czech Republic, Slovakia, Hungary, Slovenia and Croatia were part of the Austro-Hungarian Empire, part of the culture of what the Germans call *Mitteleuropa*. The Baltic States were merchant nations that traded with countries on the other side of the Baltic Sea.

But, apart from these European countries, Western-style democratisation was very much the exception globally. As the historian Frank Dikötter noted in his book *China After Mao*, nobody in China, including and especially Deng Xiaoping, ever entertained the idea of turning China into a Western democracy. The story of the liberalising Chinese leader was a myth. Chinese leaders vehemently disagreed about tactics – for example, on whether to use instruments of Western capitalism to further the goals of the Communist Party – but these were disputes about methods, not ultimate goals. Deng understood the second half of the twentieth century better than Mao. But he was not a counter-revolutionary.

After Schröder became chancellor in 1998, relations with China were even stronger than they had been under Kohl. Kohl, like Merkel later, was a reluctant neo-mercantilist. He did what he had to do, but he was never part of the CDU's corporatist circle. It was a group within that circle that tried to oust him in 1989, during a memorable party conference in the city state of Bremen. Kohl survived because he was better connected and better prepared than his opponents, including Lothar Späth, then the state premier of Baden-Württemberg. Schröder, by contrast, was a turbo-mercantilist. Like Schmidt before him, he couldn't care less about human rights. Schröder said bluntly that human rights had no place in foreign policy. He visited China six times during his chancellorship, always with large business delegations. He also made the case for China in international forums.

Angela Merkel's style was different. She would certainly not dismiss human rights with the same crassness as Schröder. But she would not place any emphasis on them either. Her period in office coincided with China's unprecedented economic transition. This is where German neo-mercantilism took off like never before. The essential characteristic of the Germany–China relationship was the interaction between the world of politics and that of business, and between these two worlds stood the lobbyists, many of them former politicians.

Karl-Theodor zu Guttenberg had been a rising star in the CSU, before he was forced to resign after a researcher found, almost by accident, that he had plagiarised his PhD thesis, copying many passages of others' work verbatim, without attribution. This is a very German scandal, as many German politicians hold PhDs of dubious pedigree, often for reasons of prestige, especially in areas such as politics, international relations or international law. A PhD used to be considered helpful to a political career, and many politicians like Guttenberg pursued their PhD work on a part-time basis. The intent was rarely to add to the sum total of knowledge. Angela Merkel is one exception: she was a physicist early in her career. As a result of the scandal, Guttenberg was forced out of office in 2011 and reinvented himself as a lobbyist.

One of his later clients was Wirecard. It was a marriage made in hell. Like Guttenberg himself, Wirecard was at one point a rising star. The German fintech company was a rare example of a newcomer making it into the DAX share index, which is mostly inhabited by the old industrial behemoths. Wirecard sold payment systems. In June 2020, it declared that €2 billion of customer money had gone missing, as had its chief executive. It was the most spectacular case of corporate fraud in modern Germany – Germany's version of Enron.

Only a year earlier, Guttenberg had intervened on behalf of his dodgy client – and he had done so directly through Merkel. The following passage, published on the FragDenStaat website, is the result of a freedom of information request:

Guttenberg asked Merkel to put in a word for Wirecard with the Chinese leadership for the acquisition of a payments licence through the purchase of a Chinese company. Guttenberg defended this as an important stimulus for the further deepening of German–Chinese financial and economic relations. Five days later, Lars-Hendrik Röller, Merkel's economic adviser, reported back to Guttenberg: 'The topic has been raised by the boss [redacted]. Please keep me informed. I will also continue to flank this.'

The 2010s were the decade of the China lobbyist. Another famous one is the former SPD leader and defence minister, Rudolf Scharping. He was found to have taken money for making a presentation, paid for by a PR company on behalf of a defence contractor. Scharping never managed to clear up whether he was already defence minister when these payments were made. He was forced out of office as a result of the scandal and became a China lobbyist. He founded a consultancy to help German companies open markets in China and vice versa. He acts as a political door-opener because of his contacts and connections to politicians in both countries. Once asked about the Chinese human-rights abuses against the Uyghurs, Scharping said, 'All chancellors, all federal governments since Helmut Schmidt have done this. We have to get out of the alleged logic of sanctions, towards a more far-sighted policy with practical results.'

For a long time, his pro-China views were very much mainstream. Even as the current government adopted more restrictive policies towards China, Scharping continued to propagate close ties with China on issues ranging from supply chains and business deals to climate change. But Scharping goes much further than mere advocacy of a realist foreign policy. He is also vehemently opposed to the idea of de-risking. It is interesting that China itself is the de-risker par excellence. The rest of the world is far more dependent on China than China is on the rest of the world. Supply-chain security has always been of utmost importance to President Xi Jinping. One reason the Germans and the Chinese get on so well in business is that they are both industrial mercantilists. But Germans like Scharping have been much more focused on business, while some of their Chinese counterparts were playing a bigger game.

Lack of geopolitical thinking is a very common trait among German political elites, because they externalise all notions of political risk. Exports are fully insured by the Hermes export credit scheme run by the government, and NATO takes care of the rest. Why bother? As long as the government continues to help pave the way to lucrative contracts, all is good.

Guttenberg and Scharping are only the tip of the iceberg. *Tagesspiegel* uncovered a whole network of German China lobbyists. Another well-known example is Hans-Peter Friedrich, a CSU politician and former German interior minister. He was active in two associations that maintain close ties with China and Chinese companies: China-Brücke – meaning 'Bridge to China' – and the Committee on German–Chinese Relations. He only declared the latter position when he no longer held it. Due to his chairmanship of China-Brücke, Friedrich had to register an interest in the lobby register of the Bundestag. Schröder's decision to work for Putin and the Nord Stream 2 consortium was not that exceptional. It was, and remains, common for senior government ministers to become political lobbyists after their careers end.

What about Olaf Scholz? As we have seen, Olaf Scholz was not a member of the pro-Putin collective that included most of the SPD's leadership. But he was in the China club – square in the middle.

The Chinese cultivated Scholz early. As mayor of Hamburg, Scholz was technically a state premier, because Hamburg is both a city and a state. Like the state premiers of the largest states, Scholz went on visits to China when he was mayor, taking local businesspeople with him, starting shortly after he got elected with a trip to Beijing and Shanghai. The Chinese gave Scholz far more attention than the mayor of a small city-state could normally expect to receive. Scholz met a vice premier, the vice foreign minister, as well as the head of the international department of the Communist Party Central Committee. One journalist opined at the time that the Chinese saw in Scholz a potential future chancellor. China is known to cultivate ties to regional politicians who can further their interests.

Scholz leads a government coalition of predominantly China-sceptic coalition partners, especially the Greens, a source of conflict. The most senior Greens leaders in the government – Robert Habeck, the economics minister, and Annalena Baerbock, the foreign minister – are both China hawks. Habeck wanted to block a Chinese investment into a terminal of the port of Hamburg; Scholz wanted the sale to go ahead. Scholz prevailed in this conflict in a compromise that restricted the Chinese investment to under 25 per cent.

But, by then, the winds of change were already blowing. Baerbock declared in a letter to ambassadors that the era of 'business first' in German politics was over. Later, she even called Xi a dictator. This is the first time that I can remember senior ministers in the German government going against the industrial lobby head on.

I agree with Baerbock that foreign policy should not be subjugated to the interests of business. But I also believe that she went too far when she personally offended a foreign leader. In diplomacy, it is essential to keep the channels open and refrain from name-calling. But she was right, in essence. The German model constituted a denial of geopolitics in the age of geopolitics.

Scholz himself gave a name to this: *Zeitenwende* – or 'change of era'. It has been the only memorable thing he has done. He was referring to Germany repositioning itself from the role of the geopolitical fence-sitter, who would do business with everybody, to a firm anchor in the Western alliance – a shift in German diplomacy, away from both Russia and China. But it did not take long for Scholz to U-turn on his U-turn. In April 2024, he reverted to his erstwhile uncritical pro-China position. Scholz was desperate to improve cooperation with China and even took the opportunity to criticise the European Commission's planned tariffs on Chinese electric cars. Scholz said the EU should act from a position of confident competitiveness, as opposed

to protectionist motives, as he put it. It is rare, and astonishing, for an EU leader to criticise EU policy while abroad.
But we are not living in normal times. What is clear is that
Scholz is breaking with the US-led China-sceptic position
of the West. After all the geopolitical disruption of the current decade, there is now a clear longing for a return to the
good old times.

But the times have changed. China is not the same
country it was when Scholz flew there for the first time.
Nowadays, it is the Chinese who are the senior partners in
the relationship.

In classic neo-mercantilist style, Scholz always had some
businesspeople in tow when he went over. In 2012 when he
was mayor of Hamburg, he took twelve entrepreneurs with
him in his plane, but interestingly there was no rush of
businesspeople eager to join the chancellor. When Merkel
travelled to China, she attracted a few more members from
the business community. A freedom of information request
revealed that she was accompanied by eighteen businesspeople during her trip to China in 2015.

The necessity for freedom of information requests is typical of the neo-mercantilist system. The German government
does not voluntarily release this information, which reveals a
system of old-fashioned patronage. Merkel helps with business contracts, the businesses help her. Neo-mercantilism is
where politics meets business behind closed doors, in what
used to be smoked-filled rooms. The same secrecy accompanied Germany–Russia relations. After Putin's invasion

of Ukraine, Steinmeier and Gabriel refused to release their notes from previous years on the grounds that it was not in the public interest.

Apart from the chancellors and the lobbyists, there is a whole industry of diplomatic-relations tourism at all levels: state secretaries travelling to China with a few businessmen in tow; mayors; state premiers. These days, the states all have their own China corporations: NRW Global Business, the Society of International Economic Cooperation of Baden-Württemberg, the Economic Development Agency of Brandenburg and, my favourite, Bayern International, which is not a football club. The biggest state is North Rhine-Westphalia, which would be a medium-sized country if it were a member of the EU, and NRW Global Business is proportionally large. In 2010, it lured businesses to put their names to the following message:

The delegation is accompanied by representatives of the North Rhine-Westphalian Ministry of Economics, which gives it a special status. The door-opening function of political accompaniment, which has already been tried and tested many times, will also contribute to the success of the trip to China. The long-standing political contacts between North Rhine-Westphalia and the Middle Kingdom will thus also benefit the companies and facilitate their entry into the Chinese market.

A record was set by the state premier of Baden-Wuerttenberg, Wilfried Kretschmann, who travelled to China with a delegation of 120 businesspeople in 2015. It is worth noting that this delegation was larger by far than that of the German chancellor Angela Merkel in the same month – let alone the twelve sad figures who accompanied Scholz in 2022. Kretschmann also took five ministers with him, and they visited the Chinese site of Taicang, home to 230 companies from his state.

All the states are at it, whether run by the left or the right. Kretschmann hails from the Greens. Lower Saxony's economics minister took four trips to China, each with big business delegations of up to thirty participants, including a visit to Huawei in 2017.

Every year, the Bavarian Ministry of Economic Affairs, together with Bayern International, offers fifteen to twenty delegation trips to new and promising markets. The focus is on the interests of Bavarian companies and their export goals. Bayern International takes care of all the travel logistics.

The German political economy is made of mirror images at federal and state level. Both see exports and a strong industry as the goal. This gives companies the option to make use of various support schemes. The dual structure also creates a competitive dynamic between states, and between a state and the federal government, which again works in favour of industry. The result is that Germany has seventeen individual relationships with China, one at federal and sixteen at state level.

The 2010s were the heyday of the China–Germany relationship, but also the decade when the first problems set in. At the beginning of the decade, China identified the

German city of Duisburg, which lies a few kilometres to the west of the Ruhr valley where I grew up, as the hub for its Belt and Road project, a giant network of roads and railways to connect the east and west of the Eurasian continent. They chose Duisburg because it has the largest inland river port in the world. In 2011, the first train on the China Railway Express arrived in Duisburg from Chongqing in south-western China – via Russia and Belarus. Thousands more followed over the years. One of them, in 2014, would carry President Xi Jinping on his state visit to Germany. That was probably the high watermark of the bilateral relationship.

China invested heavily in Duisburg. COSCO took a stake in the Duisburg port. A series of Chinese companies settled in the city, but they were mostly small traders – your classic noodle-soup exporter. What struck the Duisburgers the most was that the Chinese would never speak to them. It was a community that stuck to itself. The Germans and Chinese had planned to build a big business centre together, but abandoned those plans as China lost interest.

The venture did all right initially, but it was not the success the two sides had hoped for. Then came the pandemic and the war in Ukraine. Sanctions against Russia and Belarus meant that rail traffic had become too expensive to insure. The Belt and Road project was supposed to be the Chinese version of globalisation. China was and still is heavily dependent on rail infrastructure. Italy was China's biggest catch, but, as of late 2023, Italy was on the verge of dropping out the Belt and

Road relationship. The Duisburg link was as far as Germany ever got.

Today, this episode is symbolic of the gap between what China and especially Germany expected to happen, and what actually happened. Events intruded.

One such event was the pandemic. It brought havoc to just-in-time supply chains – so much so that German companies began to reshore parts of their production. A clothing retailer even opened a factory in Germany to produce jeans. Textile production in Europe had become one of the first victims of globalisation and the new world of just-in-time production. The pandemic brought it back, briefly. The supply-chain shock that was most economically damaging was in semiconductors. Car companies could not get their hands on semiconductors, which led to a change in policy in the EU, away from supply-chain optimisation to supply-chain security. The German government spent billions in subsidies for semiconductor manufacturing plants in Europe. De-risking had become all the rage.

Russia's invasion of Ukraine brought further supply disruptions, beyond oil and gas. German manufacturing had become heavily dependent on Russian-sourced raw materials, like palladium. Russia is the world's largest producer of this metal, a critical component in the production of fuel cells.

The US sanctions on China – starting with Huawei under President Donald Trump and followed by Joe Biden's ban on exporting high-performance semiconductors to China

– had a huge impact on Europe–China relations. The Dutch company ASML, which specialises in the production of lithography equipment that can etch pathways on to circuit boards, was forced to stop sales to China. Along with SAP and Schneider of France, it is one of the three European tech companies in the global top-fifty list. European governments had to suspend their 5G rollout, which depended strongly on Huawei equipment. German telecom operators were more dependent on Huawei than others. The German government was torn between its classic commercial relationships with China and the security interests it was forced to take seriously. For many in Germany, it was a new and disorienting experience. Geopolitics had intruded.

But this did not come suddenly. In 2011, a study by the University of Cologne had warned about the risks of global value chains. It cited the example of the Fukushimi nuclear accident in Japan in 2011, which had massive consequences for global supply chains. In Germany, it caused disruption for the metal processing industries.

But, from a German perspective, perhaps the most important intrusion of all was China's emergence as a systemic competitor to German industries. For Germany, this was the big change. China started off as a cheap place to make goods. China bought German plans and machinery to make those goods. Today, China is much further developed than Germany in areas like artificial intelligence, electric cars and some environmental technologies, like batteries, solar cells and heat pumps. China is also starting to specialise in the plant and machinery that they used to buy from Germany. Back in 2007, the mainstream view in Germany, as expressed by the chairman of the Asia-Pacific Committee of German Industry, was that China was an opportunity, not a threat. This was despite several commentators having by then already warned of the risks of Germany's increasing openness towards China.

That view changed when the Chinese took over the German solar-panel market and moved production to China. They killed off the remaining German suppliers by flooding the market with cheap panels. The solar industry had been one of Germany's success stories, but it succumbed to aggressive Chinese tactics. That was the beginning of a gradual shift in perceptions in Berlin, triggering the first industrial policy response from Merkel's economic minister, Peter Altmaier.

The relationship was not on equal terms. When German companies invested in China, they were subject to controls. They had to hand over their technical know-how to their joint-venture partner companies. In 2005, *Manager Magazin* was already expressing concern that many European jobs would be lost because of Germany's liberal China policy. It quoted a forecast according to which China would obtain a similarly prominent position in global supplies as Saudi Arabia had secured in the oil market. This is exactly what happened.

China has the unique distinction that Germany runs a trade deficit against it. China is the largest importer to

Germany, with a volume of €192 billion, but it only ranks fourth for exports, with a total value of German goods of around €107 billion. This puts China behind the USA, France and the Netherlands for exports. China seems to have the upper hand in this trading relationship. Even though Germany imports more from China than the other way around, Germany is far more dependent on China for its supply chains.

Small and medium-sized companies are particularly dependent on Chinese imports and exports, and are far less able to shift their supply chains quickly. In a survey by DZ Bank, 36 per cent of German SMEs said their supply chains were particularly dependent on China. This is mainly due to a higher dependency on Chinese wholesalers. The smaller the company, the greater the dependency. Even though the cost advantage of China is no longer what it was twenty years ago, it is significant enough. A change away from cheap Chinese goods or intermediate goods would raise costs for importers.

In 2022, German trade with China shifted dramatically. Exports went up by only 3 per cent, but imports rose by 34 per cent. There were fifteen product groups in which the share of Chinese imports has risen to over 80 per cent. In total, there are thirty-six product groups where the Chinese share is 80 per cent or more and eighty-six product groups where the share is above 70 per cent.

Despite the reports that dependence on China is not as pronounced as is often thought, this analysis paints a rather different picture. It seems that China controls important choke points for German imports, with sectors like electronics, rare earths, magnets, batteries and chemicals being particularly hit. We can draw similar conclusions, here, to those in the discussion of interdependence with Russia. Germany has become progressively more dependent on China, while China has become progressively less dependent. It has been the policy of successive Chinese governments to reduce their relative dependence on critical raw materials from the rest of the world. This has not been a priority for the Germans, who have focused mostly on maxing out business opportunities. Things got worse for Germany in the first three months of 2023, with imports down by 12 per cent, due to problems with car exports. The German car makers are struggling in the Chinese markets, which they dominated not too long ago. China has since overtaken Germany and Japan as the world's largest car exporter. Today, Germany is dependent on China for a whole range of goods – 80 per cent of laptops and 70 per cent of mobile phones are imported from China. The biggest dependencies are in rare earths, where 98 per cent of Germany's supply is imported from China, and photovoltaic systems and solar cells, where 87 per cent comes from China.

But, instead of reducing dependency, German firms are staying put. *Handelsblatt* quotes a study by the German Association of Materials Management, Purchasing and Logistics that says a withdrawal from China is out of the question for the majority of German companies. It is not just about cost. These companies simply have no physical alternatives.

The bigger problem is that China will eventually have to adjust its own internal imbalance, especially the large percentage of investments in GDP. The ideal economic response would be to shift towards consumption, but what China is doing is to shift resources to subsidise manufacturing exports. This is where it confronts Germany, and the EU at large, head on.

Germany was one of the biggest beneficiaries of China's investment-focused business model. But that era is over. As China subsidises exports, it crowds out German competitors. The main product Germany sells to China has for a long time been the motor car, but the German car makers are now all struggling in the Chinese market because the Chinese buyers prefer domestically made cars. Another factor is that Chinese households and private-sector companies currently have little confidence in the economy, and therefore very little consumption and investment is taking place.

There are still some sectors in which China is dependent on imports from Germany, where it would struggle to find alternative suppliers. This is mostly in the engineering sectors: measuring and control instruments, high-tech machines, machine tools, some medical equipment and special chemical products. There are also strong dependencies in aerospace vehicles and special pharmaceuticals as well.

China has stepped up investments in the early part of the

last decade. In 2016, there were a record 309 takeovers for a total of €86 billion. In 2022, that fell to €4 billion. Of those, the German share was only $290 million. The pandemic was clearly a factor, but the worsening geopolitical tensions ensured that the momentum before the pandemic was not regained.

An important milestone was the Chinese acquisition of the German robotics company KUKA, in 2016. This rang alarm bells with German politicians, as KUKA is a market leader in Industry 4.0 smart manufacturing. Using industrial policy, Sigmar Gabriel, economics minister at the time, tried to get other German companies to step in, making enquires to check whether Siemens or Bosch would get involved. But they rebuffed him.

Herein lies the fundamental German dilemma. Germany needs China to grow and buy German products. At the same time, China mustn't succeed too much and compete with Germany. This is now happening in the car sector. It has already happened in solar panels and robotics.

But the biggest problem is that China is increasingly asserting itself in Germany's home markets. China is the first country that has managed to challenge the Germans in some of their core areas. A study by the German Economic Institute in Cologne shows that the market share of Chinese exports of machinery and cars to the EU has risen, from 2.5 per cent in 2000 to 13 per cent in 2022, accompanied by a reduction in Germany's share, from 17.7 per cent to 15.5 per cent.

With electric cars, the situation is even more dramatic.

The European market share for Chinese cars was near zero in 2020 and went up to 8 per cent by 2023, and the European Commission estimates that this will go up further, to 15 per cent by 2025. The Commission is now planning to impose punitive tariffs on Chinese car makers because of unfair subsidies. From a German perspective, these tariffs are a double-edged sword. The Chinese will undoubtedly retaliate against European manufacturers in China – which will impact the massively overexposed German companies the most. Tariffs can protect industries, but they can't render an unsuccessful industry successful. A trade war would be a disaster for the European car industry going forward. Substantively, the Commission is right of course that Chinese firms benefit from government support on a much larger scale than European firms. That's the price China paid to establish a foothold in a new market – a market that was carelessly neglected by the established companies in Europe. But it is not as though the Europeans never subsidise anybody.

This leaves us with an important question: is Germany being outmuscled by a rival using a supercharged version of the same neo-mercantilist system? It is obvious that one country's trade surplus needs to be offset by another's trade deficit. If running a surplus is your business model, then you rely on willing accomplices elsewhere who are happy to absorb it. Luckily for Germany, such accomplices exist: the US is the biggest absorber of global surpluses; in Europe, the UK has played a similar role. But the capacity for trade deficits in eurozone countries, especially after the debt crisis of the last decade, is nowadays much reduced. Geopolitical fragmentation is also making it harder for Germany to find willing victims. If an economic superpower enters this game, it becomes much more difficult to sustain the imbalances. China has been running surpluses as part of its economic strategy. That itself is not a problem for Germany, as long as those surpluses are with others. But, increasingly, this is not the case anymore.

German neo-mercantilism has found its match, and what comes next is the backlash.

Angela Merkel's last big foreign-policy initiative was the Comprehensive Agreement on Investment (CAI) between the EU and China. It was emblematic of the older, trade-driven policy that Germany followed and tried to implement at the European level. But this time there was pushback.

Germany was heavily criticised for ignoring other EU countries. This is what Germany always did. Strong pressure from the Merkel government pushed the deal through in the final stages of the German EU presidency, but countries such as Italy, Belgium, Poland and Spain felt left out and ignored.

German industry, which invests heavily in China, was particularly interested in the agreement, hoping that it would create a level playing field, making market access easier and providing more stability for investment.

The agreement came a year after China violently suppressed protests in Hong Kong, and at a time when China's human-rights abuses against the Uyghurs and other minority groups in Xinjiang came into the media spotlight in Europe. Critics saw the agreement as a rubber stamp of the business-as-usual approach so favoured by German industry. A further problem was that China made no concessions on slave labour or investment protection.

German industry lobbied heavily for the agreement, including through the Asia-Pacific Committee, which, unusually, publicly recognised that the political situation in China was moving towards greater political control and authoritarianism. This puts German industry in a dilemma. Agreements like the CAI would not improve conditions much, potentially making firms more dependent without gaining major concessions from China. But the alternative would be a deterioration of relations, which puts investment and market access at risk.

The car industry, unsurprisingly, also welcomed the agreement as good for German manufacturing. The president of the Automobile Association advocated a ratification as soon as possible. So did the chemical industry, which has made huge investments in China.

But, curiously, Germany was no longer speaking as one on this issue. Critical voices started to intrude. At the seventeenth Asia-Pacific Conference of German Business, in 2022, the largest China investors among German companies – BASF, VW, Mercedes, BMW and Siemens – complained that they were not sufficiently represented by the Federation of German Industry, which took a clearly more critical stance on China. But it was the European Parliament that ultimately killed the agreement, or rather froze it, which amounted to the same thing. In response to EU sanctions against China over the persecution of the Uyghurs, China responded with its own sanctions programme, some of which specifically targeted a group of MEPs. In response, the European Parliament voted to put on hold any discussion of the CAI until Chinese sanctions were lifted.

This is a neat example of a particular flashpoint that embodies the changing geopolitical tides: the end of the Merkel era coincided with the advent of tougher foreign relations vis-à-vis China, both on an EU level and domestically. The rejection of one of her last actions, an attempt to pass industry-friendly foreign policy at EU level, is a potent symbol for the encroachment of geopolitics into the German model.

Merkel has said that she knew her time was up when she failed to get her big foreign-policy initiatives through. This was one of them.

The failure of the CAI was clearly not in the interests of the Chinese, either, who miscalculated when imposing sanctions on MEPs who had been openly critical of their country. The problem is that China reacts irrationally to any public criticism, especially over its human-rights standards. When a hypersensitive China meets a Europe that is full of its own virtue, amid evolving geopolitical deterioration, it is unsurprising that the bilateral relationship has turned frosty.

German business is as much to blame for its plight as

the government. A full-on insurance against geopolitical risk has produced a largely apolitical business community in Germany. The comments one reads from German CEOs are so naïve that I hesitate to reprint them here. They fall mostly in the category of wishful thinking. Belén Garijo, the managing director of the pharmaceutical giant Merck, for example, was reported by *Handelsblatt* to have said that Europe should not take sides in conflicts between the USA and China, but should build a bridge between the countries. This would help Germany as a business location. She considers decoupling from China to be completely unrealistic. The US and China cannot be allowed to create additional barriers to trade.

Who is going to stop them? Merck? The idea of German fence-sitting at a time when Europe has made itself dependent on the US for its security is laughable. It is symptomatic of a lack of political intelligence. In the past, political intelligence was not necessary to climb the greasy corporate pole. The only politics you needed to understand was how to bend the ear of the governments. If you happened to be a friend of Gerhard, you'd hit the jackpot.

Martin Brudermüller, the CEO of BASF, the company which has more stakes in the relationship with China than any other, is the biggest and certainly the loudest China fan among the German CEOs. He has come out with gushing predictions, for example that China will account for 50 per cent of the world market for chemicals by 2030, and about 75 per cent of global growth will have taken place in China by then. 'Do we want to, and can we, say goodbye to that,' he asked rhetorically.

The answer is not as obvious as he might think. Geopolitics will play a role in China's economic future. China's growth is already falling. If China were to invade Taiwan, those numbers would be blown completely out of the water. The Brudermüller scenario is the one in which the world finds its way back to globalisation. It is not the most realistic scenario.

The economic historian Adam Tooze gave a succinct definition of the problem Germany faces. The country is stuck with a twentieth-century business model, he said in an interview with *Sueddeutsche Zeitung*. 'In sociology, this is called "ontological uncertainty". Germany has historically defined itself to a considerable extent through notions of productive national labour – German *Wertarbeit*. This has been the case since the middle of the twentieth century, especially in industry. It does not make sense to many people how one can continue to maintain a society in which most people do not work "in production".'

The Kiel Institute for the World Economy criticised the German government's China policy for continuing to underestimate China's true influence in global supply chains, which makes diversification more difficult. As an example, they cited coltan production in the Democratic Republic of Congo, which has a 75 per cent global market share. Coltan is short for columbite-tantalite, a metallic ore that can, after some processing, store an electrical charge. Of the nineteen coltan mining companies in the country, fifteen are Chinese. The Chinese started to think about risk diversification long before we did.

When Scholz belatedly discovered the importance of Africa for Germany's strategic future, he went on a three-day visit that took him to Nigeria and Ghana. He came back with not a single concrete deal or project – only with a lot of ideas to reflect upon, as a journalist dryly noted.

The tone has since shifted in the German debate. BASF continues to double down on the Chinese market. In 2022, it made 14 per cent of its sales there, compared to 10 per cent in Germany. It is the largest national market for chemical products in the world. The company also made the largest investment by a German company in China, building a new integrated plant costing more than €10 billion. It is the size of an entire city. This project was announced in 2018, when geopolitical tension was already being felt. Brudermüller's China-dependent strategy has earned criticism, including among BASF investors who see it as a risk to be too dependent on the Chinese market. Brudermüller, the perennial China optimist, admitted in February 2023 that a Chinese invasion of Taiwan could lead to a total loss of business there, showing that he is aware of the risks.

As Die Welt reported, Brudermüller's unwavering commitment to China informed the way he used to deal with internal critics. Saori Dubourg, a member of the BASF board who had voted against the expansion in China, was forced out two years before he contract was up. The official statement was that Dubourg was leaving the company "on the best of terms".

Today, the dispute over China is no longer between the political left on the one side and business on the other, with the government siding with business. The dispute is within governments, within boardrooms and between shareholders. There now exists a strong business case to act much more cautiously, moving away from the recklessness with which German companies have exposed themselves to the Chinese market in the past.

The are clear parallels with Russia-centred corporate efforts to keep the German export model going at all costs, including the structure of associations and pressure groups which have been formed to defend corporate interests in China and influence political opinion to be China-friendly.

This is not a morality tale; I am not complaining about companies trying to seek business opportunities. I am also studiously avoiding the discussion of to what extent foreign policy should follow in the footsteps of twentieth-century realist diplomacy. I am generally sceptical, however, of foisting our own standards and values on to others. But I do believe that compliance with international law is something on which we should insist in our trade policies.

The fundamental problem with the German neo-mercantilist system is not related to this, however. Rather, it is about its lack of sustainability. It is simply not a good business model. My argument against neo-mercantilism is primarily one of political risk management. It is not a good idea to be dependent for your economic prosperity on industrialists like VW, with its legacy fuel cars, or on BASF, with its mass chemical production. Nor is it a good idea to be dependent on Russian gas and oil. And it certainly is not a good idea to become dependent on China.

But, unfortunately, this is what has happened.

5

Breaking the Brake

As in all countries, German macroeconomists disagree with one another about many things, but almost all of them agree that Germany is, and should remain, an industrial society. It makes no difference whether they are on the left or the right in the debate, Keynesian or neoclassicist; they all support an industry-based model. Some also support industrial export surpluses as an explicit policy goal. It is wrong to think that the latter would be a logical consequence of the former. It is possible for a country to have a large share of industry, and yet run a balanced current account. Germany is not one of those countries.

The large and persistent German current-account surplus, which peaked at over 8 per cent in the last part of the last decade, is the outstanding anomaly of German economic statistics. There is nothing particularly strange about Germany's economic growth, nor its rate of employment or unemployment. Germany has a better than average fiscal position compared with other industrial countries. But what truly stands out is the current-account surplus. And yet, in most discussions about German macroeconomics, it does not even feature. Few German economists would criticise the export surpluses or, heaven forbid, call for fiscal deficits to be offset. The surplus of the private sector could be balanced by the public sector, but that possibility lives only outside the imaginations of those who regularly engage in the German economic debate.

The further left you go in German politics, the stronger the adherence to the industrial model. When the former Left Party politician Sahra Wagenknecht split off to create her new party in early 2024, she called for the restoration of gas deliveries from Russia on the grounds that Germany is an industrial society. Industrial production is our competitive advantage, she declared. That advantage cannot be maintained without cheap gas deliveries.

If the left talks like this, who needs the right?

If you go deep into the far right, you will hear the same. The Alternative for Germany party has its strongholds in the old industrial towns of eastern Germany, where deindustrialisation started a long time ago. The more extreme the party, the more attached it tends to be to industry. But so are the large traditional parties of the centre-right and the centre-left. They are the political pillars on which corporate Germany rests. The SPD, the party of Olaf Scholz, also draws most of its voters from industry – the industrial towns of the west. The young crowd in the urban metropolitan centres, which used to support the SPD in the 1960s and 1970s, has largely migrated to the Greens. The CDU/CSU is the party of the industrial *Mittelstand*, the midsized corporate sector – the party of suburbia and the countryside.

The argument in favour of an export-led industrial model is always the same, whomever you ask: industry constitutes Germany's one big competitive advantage. 'Made in Germany' is what Germans are good at. So why not milk this? What else can we do? If it were true that industry constitutes a source of competitive advantage for Germany, I would agree. But it is just not the case anymore.

Trade is simultaneously a source wealth and welfare, and at the same time a source of political and economic dependency. It can contribute to prosperity, but also to inequality. Of the large countries in the world, Germany is among the most exposed when it comes to trade. Including services, Germany's foreign-trade ratio – the sum of exports and imports as a percentage of economic output – stood at 99 per cent in 2022, according to the World Bank. The world average is only 57 per cent. The ratios of the US and China are only 25 per cent and 38 per cent respectively. The UK, which likes to think of itself as a free-trade nation, has a ratio of only 69 per cent, a whopping thirty percentage points less than Germany. In every year since 1952, more goods have been exported from Germany than imported.

There was a joke going round years ago that the Germans were so in love with their current-account surplus that they thought everybody in the world should have one. Since the trade surpluses and deficits of all the countries must add up to zero, this is obviously not possible. If countries like Germany or China run excessively large trade surpluses, it is logically necessary that some other countries must absorb them – through offsetting deficits. My surplus is your deficit.

A country's external position against the rest of the world is recorded in the balance of payment. The current account focuses on the flow of goods, among other things. You can think of it as an extended version of the trade balance. A rule of thumb for Germany is that, when the current-account surplus disappears, as it did on a couple of occasions this century, the country is in recession. For Germany to grow, it needs a large and persistent surplus in the current account. In other words, Germany relies for its growth on other countries running offsetting current-account deficits. The US and UK, for example, have had current-account deficits for many years. But politics intrudes. In the UK, it was Brexit. In the US, it was a bipartisan turn against free trade, most prominently exemplified by Donald Trump. Trump is a phenomenon of a wider trend, but he is not responsible for the trend itself. Today's Democrats are also no longer the same as they were during the times of Bill Clinton. World politics is turning against the German model.

A popular excuse we keep hearing from the German defenders of the structural current-account surplus is that it is the result of decisions in the private sector. Nothing to do with the government. Do you want us to stop people from exporting? they ask. Or force them to import things they don't need?

Don't fall for this. It is the total balance of the private and the public sector that makes up the current account. And Germany not only runs massive surpluses in the private sector, but also, at times, in the public sector as well. It would be possible, and perfectly sustainable, for the government to raise the fiscal deficit to finance investment at home – in digital infrastructure, for example. That would, at least partially, offset the high current-account deficit, and would help with economic growth in the future. There exists no economic theory according to which the budget must balance each year. There is nothing wrong with current-account surpluses or deficits. There are no right numbers. The problem with the current-account surplus is the massive size – and the persistence.

Strangely enough, this is not debated anywhere in polite circles in Germany. Mainstream German economists, on the left and the right, are largely disinterested. I once asked a well-known economist what he thought about diversification from industry to services. That would take some of the pressure out of the current-account surplus and rebalance the economy. He thought this was a thoroughly bad idea. We don't want to end up like the UK with its dodgy financial institutions, he said. The German establishment's disdain for services, and its lack of understanding of what they are, is highly revealing. For them, the services industry is bankers and prostitutes. They call it the tertiary sector.

Just as there is little open debate among economists about

the German industry focus, the media are also complicit in nurturing existing narratives. The high current surplus is often portrayed in the German media as a success. *Die Welt* newspaper used to delight in reports that Germany had reclaimed the export world champion crown – usually a contest between Germany and China. It is meaningless to compare countries on the basis of the absolute size of their exports. The current account is one of several statistics, along with the international investment position, which one can think of as cumulative current-account balances.

Another way of thinking about a current-account surplus is through its mirror image in the financial account. A balance of payments is made up of two sides – the current account and the financial account. There is a lot more in it, like flows of investment, but current and financial accounts are what reflect the flow of and payment for goods and services. A surplus in a country's current account is offset by a deficit in the financial account. A deficit in the financial account means that more is being saved than invested.

If Germany sells more than it buys, it means it is a net investor abroad. Unlike many developing countries, Germany does not have a sovereign wealth fund that would manage those external surpluses. Instead, companies, the originators of those surpluses, have reinvested them abroad. That would be a great choice if they had invested in sectors or technologies they were not exposed to. But this is not what happened. German car companies invested in car factories. They could have invested some of their huge profits in companies that make electric cars or batteries. If they were really smart, they could have invested in public transport. You cannot fault someone for who they are: VW will never be Tesla. But they could have hedged their bets by investing wisely. If you define yourself as a Luddite from the analogue era, you can still benefit from new technology by becoming a silent investor in the digital world. What you don't want to do is to double down on your exposure. The idea is to manage risk through diversification.

When we celebrate Germany's export success, we are essentially celebrating an economic imbalance. But, much worse than this, we are celebrating a political dependency as I described in previous chapters. Export success is not linked to character, but to an economic model. When a country relies on exports for its livelihood, it will not see Putin for who he is, but as the guy who speaks fluent German, with old-school manners, who dances with the Austrian foreign minister at her wedding. This is what a structurally high current-account surplus does to people. They end up inviting a dictator to their wedding, or making him godfather to their children, as Gerhard Schröder did.

Occasionally, critical voices of the current strategy break through, on the right and the left. Veronica Grimm, a member of the Council of Economic Experts, broke a taboo when she said in 2023 that energy-intensive companies had no future in Germany. Subsidising their energy costs, which was being discussed at the time, would not make long-term economic sense, she argued.

Grimm's comment is not mainstream in the German debate, not even among those on the right. Nor is anything that I have been writing in this book. If you shout into a room that we must strengthen the competitiveness of German industry, you will see a lot of nodding heads. If, however, you suggest, as I do here, that Germany needs to prepare for a post-industrial future, you will be treated as somebody who does not understand how the real world works.

The current-account surplus is the most noticeable part of Germany's economic statistics. It is the expression of German exceptionalism. It informs the way Germans think about economic policy, something that constitutes a source of incomprehension among foreign observers. For this exceptionalist industrial model to work, Germany requires a macroeconomic policy infrastructure that is highly attuned to the task – with a central bank that is focused on price stability exclusively, and a fiscal policy that runs on autopilot. It is the iron-clad version of macroeconomic stability that ensures the competitiveness of industry. German economic policy's primary objective is not to maximise welfare, but to protect the business model of industry. Unfortunately, this is the model the eurozone inherited when it started the monetary union.

This ideology has a name: ordo-liberalism, a mixture of laisser-faire economics, but enshrined in a legalistic framework. It has its origins in the economic system Germany adopted after the Second World War, under Ludwig Erhard, the country's legendary economics minister. Erhard was the political front-end of a group of liberal economists who were persecuted by the Nazis, and who drew up a liberal economic order. Its most prominent member was Walter Eucken. Eucken's ordo-liberalism was distinctly different from the liberalism of Friedrich Hayek, the Austrian economist, whose ideas later became the cornerstone of market liberalisation in the US under Ronald Reagan and the UK under Margaret Thatcher. German ordo-liberalism was much more focused on industry itself, and on industrial competition and competitiveness. In this sense, it was as much an economic as a legal system, embedded deeply into constitutional law. It was a framework suited to industrial companies that competed with one another. It was not a system conducive to disruptive technologies, let alone a system in which disruptive companies could thrive. For example, it defined anticompetitiveness in terms of market shares, and resisted the intrusion of modern ideas about competition economics. It was tailor-made for the only economic structure Germany had ever known – one where companies made physical things and sold them.

What Erhard and his successors did was to complement ordo-liberalism with a social system that would give workers – and the trade unions, as their official representatives – legally enshrined rights. What set Germany apart from other countries was the right to co-determination. This meant that companies above a certain size had to accept works councils as official representatives. The unions were fully represented on companies' supervisory boards, which hired and fired the chief executives.

The macroeconomic counterpart of this system was a stability-oriented fiscal and monetary policy – based on strict and legally enshrined rules. The Bundesbank Act of 1957 granted the German central bank independence and gave it a mandate to pursue price stability at the expense of all other objectives. The Federal Reserve, the US central bank, by contrast, has a dual mandate: price stability and high levels of employment.

The counterpart to a stability-focused monetary policy was a stability-focused fiscal policy, geared towards balanced budgets. The idea was to prevent a build-up of debt that would have to be funded later through higher taxes. The system included so-called automatic stabilisers like unemployment insurance. When the economic cycle turns down, tax receipts fall and spending on unemployment rises. The Germans were OK with that. But they objected to active fiscal stimulus until very recently. Stimulus is alien to the German culture.

You could call the German system an attempt to do economics through the legal system. There were more lawyers in the finance ministry than economists. I once had a discussion with a former head of the federal cartel office, long after he had retired, and asked him about what he thought of modern competition economics. He was a lawyer by profession. He told me he had made it his job the keep the economists out.

Monetary union was where the force of European integration and modern economics clashed with the mindset of

German ordo-liberalism. During the negotiations for the Maastricht Treaty, Germany insisted on the principle of central bank independence and an exclusive mandate of price stability, enshrined in a much stricter legal principle even than the system Germany operated at home. Central bank independence in Germany was not part of the constitution. It was an ordinary law that could have been overturned by a simple majority. No one ever dared. But since the Germans mistrusted everyone else in Europe, they insisted that central bank independence would have to be part of the treaty – along with fiscal rules.

In the process, they goofed. The fiscal target they chose was based on averages at the time. Back in early in the 1990s, the average debt-to-GDP ratio was 60 per cent. The annual nominal growth of GDP was 5 per cent – 'nominal' means in terms of actual money, not corrected for inflation. If you multiply 5 per cent by 60 per cent, you get 3 per cent. This is exactly the 3 per cent deficit limit. If you stick to a maximum deficit of 3 per cent and if you keep growing at 5 per cent nominally, you should keep your debt-to-GDP stable – at around 60 per cent, if this is where you started. This is fine as a guide, but they put these numbers into the treaty. They did not consider that the world would change.

European countries are no longer growing at 5 per cent nominally. Debt-to-GDP ratios are much higher, and many countries, including Italy and France, will never get them down to 60 per cent. When the German government realised in the mid-1990s that the fiscal targets would not be enough, they insisted on another law to enforce them. This became known later as the Stability and Growth Pact. The idea was that governments with a high debt-to-GDP ratio would run fiscal surpluses to get government debt to the 60 per cent target. Most of the disputes at the time were about exceptions, for example during recessions.

German industry supported the idea of a monetary union as a complement to a single market. The efficiency of a large domestic market was important to them. The German ordo-liberal policy elite in the Bundesbank, the central bank, and the finance ministry was much more cautious, bordering on the Eurosceptic.

This was 1998, and the tail end of the long reign of Helmut Kohl. The Stability and Growth Pact was agreed at a finance ministers' meeting in Dublin, in a peace deal brokered by Kenneth Clarke, who was then the UK's Chancellor of the Exchequer. Later that year, Kohl lost the election to Gerhard Schröder. After sixteen years in opposition, the SPD returned to power.

But it was no longer the same SPD as that of Helmut Schmidt, who in 1979 agreed at a G7 meeting that Germany would act as a global economic locomotive through a big increase in the fiscal deficit. Back then, Keynesians like Schmidt were still in charge in the SPD. During the 1990s, the SPD took a distinctly conservative turn in its fiscal policy. Social Democrats have become paranoid about being castigated as profligate and incompetent in all things related to money, a legacy of the political battles in the 1970s. This is despite the party having had some of the most competent finance ministers in Germany's history, including Helmut Schmidt himself and Professor Karl Schiller in the early part of the 1970s. During that decade, the SPD followed a Keynesian economic policy, as did many left-of-centre parties did in those days. By the 1980s, fiscal conservatives had taken over everywhere. Whether in academia or in politics, this was the age of the conservative resurgence.

In 1998, the SPD's trend towards fiscal conservativism was briefly interrupted when Oskar Lafontaine, the SPD chairman, became finance minister under Schröder. He was in office for only a few months, when one day he suddenly quit as finance and party chairman. It was one of the most mysterious moments in modern German politics. Lafontaine was one of the big beasts of German politics at the time. I got to know him well during that time and had several conversations with him on how the newly created eurozone should work. He was that rare species of a German Keyensian, an advocate of more government spending for investment. Schröder, by contrast, was a fiscal conservative who believed in corporatist deals. Lafontaine never spoke about this episode in detail, except to make it clear that he disagreed with what he considered Schröder's neoliberal policies. After a cabinet meeting in which Schröder was open critical of Lafontaine's policies, Lafontaine quit on 11 March 1999. He did not meet with Schröder. There was no press conference. Lafontaine wrote a letter simply to say that he resigned from all political offices - finance minister, party chairman, and his seat in the

Bundestag – and disappeared from view. He resurface as joint leader of the Left Party in 2005, but later quit that party as well. In 2015, he married Sahra Wagenknecht in 2015, who quite the Left Party in 2023 to form her own party, BSW, a populist party of the left with themes of the right.

After Lafontaine quit his job as finance minister in 1999, he was succeeded by Hans Eichel, the former premier of the state of Hesse and a far more orthodox figure on the right of the party. I would not characterise him as a fully paid-up member of fiscal conservatism. It was during his reign that Germany, together with France, broke the EU's fiscal rules and was subjected to an excessive-deficit procedure. Eichel explained that he needed to run a higher deficit to pay for economic reforms, an argument that always appeared sensible to me. The hypocrisy was that Germany claimed a flexibility for itself that it denied to others.

The Schröder years were a difficult period for Germany – the 'sick man of Europe' episode. Economic performance was dire. Schröder started the reforms in 2003, but never reaped the benefits. He narrowly lost the 2005 elections and left active politics. I argued at the time that one of the reasons for Germany's disappointing economic performance in that period was that it had entered the monetary union at an overvalued exchange rate. Unification had left a financial toll, yet that was not reflected in intra-EU exchange rates. France and Italy had both devalued in the 1990s.

Eventually, the German economy adjusted through the labour market. Schröder's reforms had incentivised trade unions and employers to negotiate moderate wage agreements. In turn, wage moderation increased German competitiveness within the eurozone.

When the Schröder government lost power in 2005, and Angela Merkel formed a grand coalition with the SPD as the junior partner, another Social Democrat became finance minister: Peer Steinbrück. Unusually for a German finance minister, he was a Eurosceptic, and he torpedoed European responses to the financial crisis. His lasting legacy was the debt brake – probably the worst fiscal rule by any government anywhere. We should always remember when discussing this monster of a debt rule that it was invented by the SPD.

Still reeling from the 2003 episode when Germany was subjected to an embarrassing excessive-deficit procedure, the left and right huddled together to agree a completely new framework for fiscal policy at the federal and state level. In 2007, they created a federal commission, made up representatives of the states and the government, to work out a new constitutional fiscal rule. The final agreement on the debt brake came in 2009 when the Bundestag and the Bundesrat, the two chambers of the German parliament, voted in favour with the required two-thirds majorities.

The debt brake is in some respects a logical continuation of the EU's Stability and Growth Pact, but in reality it turned into a fiscal doomsday machine. The Stability Pact, on which Germany had insisted, and which Germany later broke, never became an effective operational fiscal framework. It had a certain 'tomorrow I shall be sober' quality, even when the rules were toughened in 2005 with the first of several Stability Pact reforms. What Germany tried to do with its constitutional debt brake is to translate the Stability Pact's lofty ambitions into a proper fiscal framework. But, importantly, this was an entirely national policy. There was no coordination with the rest of the EU: they had the Stability Pact; Germany had the debt brake.

One of the astonishing aspects of the debt brake was the degree of consensus for it. The SPD had moved so far to the right by then, under Steinbrück as finance minister, that even the golden rule to maintain the level of net investments was considered fiscally profligate.

The debt brake was a complex construction. It did not just set targets, like the Maastricht Treaty, or a vague aspiration, like the original Stability and Growth Pact, but it went into excruciating procedural and legal detail. It is very much an outgrowth of German ordo-liberalism, the attempt to subject economic policy to a complete set of rules. The idea is to prevent any economic arguments from entering the discussion. The debt brake imposes a limit for annual deficits: 0.35 per cent of GDP. It has a cyclical component: during recessions, governments do not have to cut back when tax revenues fall and when welfare costs increase. It also comes with a piggy bank – a virtual account that registers overshoots and undershoots. If the government achieves a surplus in one year, it can use it for spending in other year. It is a true piggy bank in the sense that the savings have to be built up first. In practice, it never worked like this. This is the piggy bank that likes to say *No*.

The debt brake allowed governments and the parliament to declare fiscal emergencies, such as during a pandemic, or after an environmental catastrophe. This happened, justifiably so, when COVID-19 struck in 2020. The debt brake remained suspended for four years. So did the EU's Stability Pact. The question everybody asked during that period was whether it marked the end of the mechanism. I heard brave forecasts, usually from economists on the left, who were certain that there was no way the Germans would ever be able to comply with their own fiscal rules. What they overlooked was that Germany's willingness and ability to engage in fiscal restraint is legendary – even if it makes no economic sense.

The debt brake also applied to the state governments. Their dire fiscal situation was one of the primary reasons for the federal reform of the previous decade. The rule formally took effect in 2016 – with a longer transition period for the states. But the debt brake was de facto applied informally shortly after it was agreed.

The economists Peter Bofinger and Gustav Horn, both on the Keynesian side of the German political debate, argued in 2007 that the German economy was already constrained by the monetary union. Because of its dependence on exports, Germany was much more susceptible to global shocks than the US, for example, and would therefore require more countercyclical fiscal policies to stabilise the economy during a crisis. That argument made sense to me. The two economists were not against a fiscal framework. On the contrary, they favoured the golden rule, under which the government was still allowed to borrow to fund investments. The debt brake came without a golden rule. It did not discriminate between spending and investment.

The worst consequence of the debt brake became apparent during the eurozone debt crisis, beginning in 2009, which led to a fall in net investments. Whenever governments imposed austerity, they always ended up cutting net investments. That is a consequence of how democracies work. A lot of government spending is non-discretionary. Social transfers, or defence spending, cannot be interrupted during a recession. Investments that don't get made don't scream as loudly as welfare recipients or taxpayers. When austerity is imposed, investment is what gets hit first. As Germany imposed austerity on itself, it essentially forced other countries in the eurozone to do the same. Everyone did it at the same time, and everyone underestimated the consequences of synchronised austerity.

Bofinger and Horn wanted to set minimum spending targets for education and the protection of the environment. Proponents of the debt brake often invoked the interests of future generations, that they oughtn't be burdened with the debt of their forebears – the classic argument of fiscal conservatives. The counterargument is that we do more harm to them if we save on education or infrastructure.

In June 2009, I wrote in my *Financial Times* column that the 0.35 per cent deficit limit was economically illiterate and would lead to lower investments. That is pretty much what happened. What I did not see at the time was the consequences this would have for the future of the German economic model, the main subject of our story here.

The golden rule is a sensible rule, and demonstrably so. A decade earlier, the UK chancellor, Gordon Brown, introduced a new medium-term fiscal-policy framework that included the golden rule to borrow in order to fund investments and a set of other fiscal rules. While the UK is not a shining example of solid economic management, that part of the fiscal governance framework has worked very well. Yet, many German economists, including the powerful Council of Economic Experts, rejected the golden rule as an incarnation of evil. Bofinger himself was a long-standing member of the council, the eternal minority voice in that five-member committee.

The data since have showed that Germany suffered a reduction in net capital stock during the period between 2005 and 2015 – and ranked close to the bottom in international comparisons, according to the economists Michael Hüther and Jens Südekum. This criticism was shared by many, especially non-German, economists. Outwardly, an uber-competitive Germany looked like a successful economy, but the rot had already set in.

While economists disagreed, at least to some extent, there was universal acceptance of the debt brake across the political spectrum. This goes to show that, in Germany, the economic debate and the political one are often disconnected. The only dissenting voices in the political arena were the Left Party and the Greens. The Greens saw the debt brake as a hindrance to their green-investment programme – rightly so, as it later proved to be the case. The Left Party was mostly concerned with social transfers and regarded the debt brake as a mechanism to redistribute income from the poor to the rich.

The year of the debt brake was also the year of the post-financial-crisis recession and continued stress in the banking sector. Steinbrück vetoed plans by the European Commission for an EU stimulus programme on the grounds that it would have to be bankrolled by Germany. But he was more generous in bailing out domestic banks that were part of the SPD power network. By the end of the year, the economy had started to recover, and a few months later, Steinbrück's successor, Wolfgang Schäuble, reported higher than expected tax revenue, but warned that the country should maintain its consolidation course.

In 2009, another story developed in parallel – in Greece. During that year, it became increasingly clear that Greece was heading for trouble. Eurointelligence, a web publication I co-founded, had already warned, in January of that year, that the dismissal of the finance minister was a sign of a potential default later. By April, Eurostat, the EU statistics office, had warned that the deficit would rise to 4.8 per cent. That was considered a shocking number at the time, but it would get much worse. The country held elections later that year, from which the opposition PASOK party, under the new leader George Papandreou, emerged victoriously. PASOK's new finance minister shortly afterwards announced that the 2009 deficit figure would be 12.9 per cent, with public debt now up to over 110 per cent of GDP. Horrified by those numbers, the European Commission called for a full investigation. This was the beginning of what later became known as the eurozone crisis.

This book is not about that crisis, but it plays into our theme. This was the phase in our recent economic history when Germany was doing comparatively well relative to other countries. These were the years when Germany strengthened its global competitiveness. The decline of the euro's exchange rate played an important role. In July 2008, the euro had hit an all-time high against the US dollar, of 1.59 dollars to the euro. By February 2015, the euro was down to 1.12 dollars. In 2022, it fell briefly below parity and has since recovered a little. In dollar terms, the fall between 2008 and 2015 constituted a 40 per cent nominal devaluation.

One reason currencies devalue against one another is inflation. That was not the case here. European inflation in that period was much lower than in the US. Indeed, by 2015, the eurozone was on the verge of deflation, prompting the ECB to start a programme of quantitative easing, the purchase of government and corporate bonds. The goal was to raise the level of inflation. What the eurozone therefore experienced was a massive real exchange depreciation of some 40–50 per cent. But the benefits were not evenly distributed. The biggest beneficiaries were the eurozone's largest exporters – Germany and the Netherlands. All of this was happening while trade unions went through a phase of wage moderation. The generation of baby boomers had reached an age at which they valued continued employment so much that they were willing to sacrifice wage rises. German workers had, all of a sudden, become risk averse. Workers in their mid-fifties, already with a view to retirement, behaved differently than they had when they were striking in favour of the thirty-five-hour week during the 1990s.

There was another factor that benefited Germany in that period. The eurozone crisis turned German government bonds into safe-haven assets. The German government bond had become the eurozone's de facto sovereign bond. The bond spread always had the German ten-year bond as the benchmark. German bunds, as they are called, carry the lowest interest rates. With quantitative easing, medium- to long-term interest rates were also pushed lower. This in turn produced a credit boom in Germany, especially in housing and construction, a market that had previously laid dormant for decades. All the ingredients of a massive economic boom were in place – low interest rates, competitive wages, high export surpluses and a real exchange devaluation of a magnitude that does not come often.

The financial media abroad started to sing the praises of Germany's reborn miracle economy. A little while later, when Donald Trump became president, Angela Merkel was eulogised as the true leader of the Western world. Liberals everywhere looked at Germany as an alternative model, politically and economically. They did not look under the bonnet.

They did not see, or did not want to see, that the policies of the German government were hardly changed from those of decades earlier. Germany was building ever closer ties with Russia, interrupted only briefly by Russia's annexation of Crimea in 2014. Sanctions followed, but Merkel maintained an open dialogue with Putin. Throughout most of her time in office, she was indeed the most accomplished political leader in Europe, and one of the few who read her briefs. She is probably the most informed politician I have ever met. In previous decades, we had Margaret Thatcher in the UK and Bill Clinton in the US who had a similar command of details. In the politics of Merkel's period, that quality was quite rare.

The first phase of the euro crisis ended in 2012 when Mario Draghi, president of the European Central Bank, uttered the now legendary words that he would do 'whatever it takes' to save the euro. That ended the sovereign debt crisis, which flared up briefly again in 2015, when Greece was on the verge of default unless it accepted another EU bailout programme, and the conditions that came with it. That was indeed a scary moment, but it was not existential to the future of Europe. A Greek default, back in 2010 when the problems first surfaced, would have ruffled feathers. But it would have been a blip. It was the attempt by the eurozone's leadership to avoid the default, while simultaneously imposing austerity, that caused the crisis to spread.

What worries me today about the future of eurozone is not another Greek crisis, but something altogether more alarming. France and Germany have started to drift apart on several fronts. France has always been focused on nuclear energy more than Germany, but the divergence became total when Germany phased out nuclear energy in April 2023. In fiscal policy, France is on course for another year of rising deficits and debt in 2024, with the deficit – as seen from the beginning of the year – on course to reach 5.4 per cent, similar to the figure for 2023. By that time, France's deficit will not have been compliant with the Maastricht Treaty for ten years. During this same period, Germany has consolidated its budget. As the French debt ratio lingered at 110 per cent, with a clearly rising tendency, the German debt ratio was 65 per cent of GDP, due to fall to below 60 per cent within a short period of time.

Good will permitting, it is always possible to solve a debt crisis in a small periphery nation. But a divergence between France and Germany is a different story. France is too big to fail, and too big to save. There is no way that Germany, having forced stringent deficit cuts on itself by sacrificing net investment, would bail out a country that did not. The ECB has a bailout programme in place, called the Transmission Protocol Instrument, but it's unlikely to be appropriate for France. This is a programme meant for countries that are following the rules and that are relatively small. France did not follow the rules, but managed to fly under the radar, in the shadow of Germany, helped by the rating agencies' benevolence.

As we saw in Greece, and with the US subprime mortgages

before that, fortunes can change quickly. Franco-German divergence constitutes a large and foreseeable crisis. There would be no good options available in such a situation. But this crisis, foreseeable though it is, may not happen in the next few years. The unsustainable is either rendered sustainable, or it comes to an end. But the unsustainable can persist for a long time. Another eurozone crisis is always a possibility, but the crisis of the German industrial model is already a reality today.

Everything that supported the German economy in the previous decade has since turned against it. The pandemic exposed vulnerable supply chains; US and French plans for reindustrialisation are happening in part at Germany's expense; the technological gap is becoming problematic, especially in the car industry; and, after the retirement of a large chunk of the baby boomers, German trade unions have become much less fearful of strike action.

The winds of technology and politics have turned not only against German industry, but against the entire ordo-liberal economic model – the banks, the industrial companies, the export surpluses and the debt brake. It all hangs together – and, together, it is not sustainable. It will have to end. But it has not ended yet.

6

We and the Others

One would think that a country with a large industrial export sector that was suffering from skilled labour shortages would be particularly welcoming to foreign workers. Or to Germans who were returning home after several years abroad. This is not so. Although Germany's policymakers understand the problems and have gone some way to redress them, it is not working on the ground.

Take, for example, the two German university professors who worked at a good university in the UK and were head-hunted for a job at the University of Leipzig. The university wanted to establish an internationally oriented degree programme, taught in English. The two professors were the top candidates.

In one case, it was just the money. The salary and civil-service status of professors and teachers in Germany are non-negotiables. At €7,000 per month, the pay was much lower than in the UK, so the first professor turned down the job. The second professor, however, accepted the salary cut and was ready to go. But the next hurdle was to find a school for his daughter.

They agreed on a state school, but the state of Saxony has a two-tier system: grammar schools, where children can earn a high-school degree – *Abitur*, as it is known in Germany – and a lower-school system, where children typically leave at the age of sixteen to take up an apprenticeship. Children who have previously been to a foreign school are automatically put into the lower-tier school system for the fifth until the ninth years. This means that the state of Saxony denies children who have attended a school abroad an academic career from the outset. The presumption is that you must be educationally disadvantaged when you come from abroad. There is a hardship clause, as they call it, whereby a student who can pass four aptitude tests in different subjects will be granted an exception, but each test has to be passed with an A grade. This is a requirement that goes well beyond the requirement for German students who want to enter they higher-tier system, and it is obvious discrimination. The second professor's loyalty to his daughter exceeded his loyalty to the state of Saxony.

A second example comes from Maria Theresa Thelen, who helps Brazilians find their way through the maze of securing employment and visas in Germany. One of her clients held a PhD in chemistry, but his German was not as impeccable as would be required for a senior-level job in Germany. His English was fluent. He applied for a mid-ranking engineering job, but was refused on the grounds that he was overqualified. But his German, which was reasonable but not perfect, disqualified him from higher-ranking jobs. He left for the Netherlands, where language was not an issue, and he found a job in a very short time.

Another of Thelen's clients held a doctorate in biology, and she was also deemed overqualified – her application for a lab job was rejected on the grounds that her qualifications would intimidate her colleagues. It took her three years to find a job in the German labour market.

A third client, also from Brazil, was asked during an interview whether she danced the samba. Even in jobs were Portuguese and Spanish language skills were advantages, candidates were commonly rejected in favour of Germans with lower qualifications. One Brazilian pharmaceutical consultant who lived in Switzerland was planning to move to Germany, where her partner lived. The German system was so obstructive that she ended up going to the UK, and only managed to get into Germany after a UK company posted her there.

I make no claim that these stories are in any way representative, and there are numerous exceptions to the rule. Germany remains one of the most attractive destinations for low-skilled immigrants but fails to attract the high-skilled immigrants it needs to sustain its model, or diversify away from it. This is the focus of this chapter. It is not about immigration in general.

The problem with language is a big one. Germany has

the disadvantage that not many immigrants speak German. Spain's experience with immigration is largely positive because many immigrants speak Spanish. Language is the reason why immigration has been so much more success-ful in the UK, especially in the large metropolitan areas like London, where immigrants now outnumber British natives. Since Brexit, however, the situation in the UK has deteri-orated, including for skilled workers. But the problems in Germany are not just about language, nor are they only policy-related – although that, too, is a problem. In fact, Germany's issues attracting skilled immigrants are largely cultural.

It starts early in life. Teachers, and especially their elected representatives, are at the most conservative and sometimes bigoted end of the debate. Heinz-Peter Meidinger, head of the German Teachers' Association, has called for a maximum ceiling on the number of immigrant children, as he believes that, when a class has 35 per cent or more children from immi-grant families, the performance of the whole class declines. An 'immigrant' is widely defined as anyone who is not born in Germany. As if this were not enough, he also wants pri-mary schools to stop teaching English, on the grounds that it is hard enough for children to learn German. The level of ignorance in these ideas is mindboggling. Children have the capacity to learn two or even three languages concurrently. The two or three days per week of English tuition is not going to impair their ability to absorb the German language, which they mainly learn at home, in any case.

Superficially, German universities are doing better than they used to in attracting students. In the 2022/3 academic year, there were 458,210 international students, out of a total of 2.9 million, at German universities. Ten years earlier, the number was only 260,000. Germany is attractive because it has prestigious universities, relatively low entrance requirements and low tuition fees. But, as we saw in the case of the professors who tried, and failed, to the re-enter the university sector, the system as a whole is not competitive.

I will offer, here, an example from my own family. After leaving school, my son briefly considered applying to a German university. He had all the required subjects and grades. But the university insisted on the successful completion of a German language course, which had to be taken in Germany. This was despite the fact that he is a German citizen.

As we saw in the example of the German professor who struggled to get his daughter into a school, Germany is a society with built-in discrimination. This is not racism. They discriminate against Germans, too. This is a not-made-in-Germany problem. The state of Saxony wrongly assumes that schools abroad do not teach to the same standard – an absurd notion, given the persistently falling international rankings of German schools in the regular PISA studies. Why does a German university even bother with gold-plated German language tests? Why would a foreign student want to attend a university course and risk not understanding a word by refusing to learn the language? It is in the student's own interest, so why not sit back and let the students do what they need to do? Do they fear the usual question from BBC correspondents in European capitals: 'Can you please say this in English?' This is not what students do.

Will Kymlicka, a Canadian political scientist, describes successful migration policy in terms of hardware – by which he means institutions, laws, education, formal qualifications – and software – the informal norms and attitudes that a society has towards migration and specific groups of migrants. Both factors together influence how migration plays out within a country, as they provide a framework for the opportunities and actions of migrants.

This articulates quite well what is going on in Germany. The hardware – the laws – is not too bad. It is not optimal, but it is catching up. The problem in Germany is the software. Even though Germany is a country with a high percentage of migrants or descendants of migrants, it does not feel like it, nor does it like to style itself as such. This is a clear consequence of previous attitudes and policy, which have culminated in many cultural and societal factors that inhibit migration or make migrants in Germany feel less accepted.

All of this now interacts with our main subject – the decline of the German economic model. One could at least explain elitist attitudes if a country benefits from an oversupply of labour, as was the case twenty years ago. But this is no longer so. If you ask German companies or economic institutes about the biggest structural problem facing the economy, they will cite skills shortages.

A report by the Institute of the German Economy in Cologne, which focused on labour market trends, showed that the jobs gap grew to a record 633,000 in 2023. These were unfilled jobs. The figure was only 138,000 in 2013, meaning that growth has more than quadrupled in just ten years. This trend is strongest among highly qualified workers, where the gap has widened from 68,000 to 277,000 in that period.

For skilled workers with vocational training, the gap widened from 83,000 to 355,000. Unemployment among this group has fallen by 44 per cent in the last ten years. For the low skilled, the trend has gone in the other direction. Unemployment has gone up. Germany has a lot of immigration, but of the wrong kind.

Would one not expect Germany to become more welcoming to skilled immigrants and to returning émigrés? A large percentage of the companies surveyed in various sectors state that they feel restricted by the shortage of skilled labour. The service sector is the most affected, where 54.2 per cent of companies surveyed said they suffered skills shortages, followed by manufacturing at 44.5 per cent. It is interesting that the automotive industry is below average, at 30.5 per cent.

Notably, the major German industries are less affected than the average. This fits in with our overriding theme. There is industrial bias in the labour market as well. The diversification away from the industry-based neo-mercantilist model would require more highly skilled immigration.

But the labour is heavily tilted towards the skills needed to service German industry. This is a different skill set.

As I wrote in Chapter 1, the German financial sector sucks the oxygen out of the air for company start-ups, as German politicians strategically channel national savings into old industries. The same is happening in the labour market, where resources are systemically steered towards large industrial companies. This prevents diversification.

As an aside: German vocational training is widely admired around the world, because the system produces excellently trained craftspeople. But it cannot adjust to new types of jobs that spring up spontaneously, because there is no existing training infrastructure. The car mechanic is now called a *Mechatroniker*, a bit of a mouthful even to a German who is used to these double-decker words that try to conflate two things – in this case, mechanics and electronics. The modern electric car is so different in nature, that one can easily identify the skills mismatch. The nature of jobs is changing so fast that the German vocational system is struggling to keep up. This is a world in which transferable skills matter more than highly specialised training.

For some companies, the skills shortages are getting quite serious, even to the extent that industrial companies have had to close assembly lines because they could not find workers. Some restaurants did not reopen after the pandemic because they could not find waiting staff. There is also an acute shortage of skilled labour in the public sector. By 2030, 1.3 million public-sector employees will have retired. The baby boomers are gradually booming into retirement. There are currently already 360,000 vacancies in the public sector, including in the police, schools and daycare centres.

Another survey has found that every second company cannot fill its apprenticeship positions. In 2002, Germany had the very opposite problem – the government had to strong-arm industry into absorbing an entire year of school-leavers into the apprenticeship system.

There are 100,000 fewer school-leavers per year now than there were ten years ago. Soon, Germany will be in a position where the number of people leaving the labour market will exceed the number of those joining by 400,000 each year. This is the net gap that Germany needs to fill with immigration.

You would think that German companies might at least adjust their recruitment policies. But the examples we have cited above show that this is not the case. There are three groups within the country with potential for alleviating the shortage of skilled workers if they could be integrated into the labour market: young women, workers over sixty and, as they say in Germany, people with a migration background. Currently, these groups are mostly untapped.

Post-war Germany relied on migrants from the guest-worker generation in the 1950s and 1960s. These migrants came from countries with which Germany had struck agreements for labour migration – like Italy, Spain, Greece, Turkey, Morocco, Portugal, Tunisia and Yugoslavia – in order to fill vacancies in German industry, such as the coal and steel industries of the Ruhr region, or the docks in the north of Germany.

The work was temporary and based on a principle of rotation, in which guest workers were meant to leave after a fixed number of years, when their jobs would be passed on to new arrivals. In practice, many settled in Germany. This was possible because the obligation to return home was rarely enforced, and was usually not desired by employers who had invested in training the workforce. The creation the European Economic Community, the forerunner of today's EU, established the principle of freedom of movement, so migrants from other member states enjoyed permanent rights of residency.

But guest workers faced strong discrimination in German society. Certain bars and restaurants would refuse admittance to Italians, for example, in the 1950s. Workplace discrimination was also extremely common.

From the start of the bilateral agreements in 1955 to the end of guest-worker migration in 1973, the number of migrants in Germany increased from 80,000 to 2.6 million. A total of 14 million guest workers came to Germany in that period, most of whom returned to their home countries.

Due to rising unemployment after the oil shock of 1973, and increased fears of too many foreigners, chancellor Willy Brandt put a stop to the recruitment of guest workers. As a result, many migrants created permanent roots in the country, as they would not be able to return once they had left. In 1981, Chancellor Helmut Schmidt declared bluntly: 'It was a mistake to bring so many foreigners into the country.' Helmut Kohl's government in the 1980s offered a payment of 10,500 Deutschmarks to foreign workers if they left Germany. In 1982, he said: 'Integration is only possible if the number of foreigners living with us does not continue to rise.'

From the mid-1970s until the early 2000s, the government's official line was that Germany was not an immigration country. The legal framework sought to prevent migrants from fully accessing the labour markets. But migrants with permanent residence permits, granted after five years of residence, had full access to the labour market.

In 2000, the SPD/Greens government introduced a German version of a green card, because of an increasing labour shortage in the technology and telecommunications sector, an industry whose growth Germany had slept through. This was the first time since the introduction of the guest-worker programme that policy on migration had shifted towards encouraging migrant workers to come to Germany. Over the years since, Germany has moved closer to a model similar to that of Canada and the USA.

However, the green-card system, well intended as it was, did not work. Its underlying tone was still based on a fear of migrants. Notably, it only focused on the IT profession. It also excluded the partners of IT professionals from the labour market for at least two years upon arrival, and it limited the work permit to a period of five years. Consequently, its quantitative impact was low. The goal of issuing 20,000 green cards was never reached. By 2003, the number of cards issued only ran into the hundreds. By contrast, Germany had never had problems attracting low-skilled workers, which was what informed their policies. But they applied the same principles to high-skilled workers, as though highly skilled computer scientists were queuing up outside the borders, begging to be let in.

The 2005 Immigration Act saw some liberalisation, with less bureaucracy for visa processing once workers had a job offer. This simplified applications from foreign entrepreneurs, for example, and made it easier for foreign students to go to German universities and to stay in Germany to seek a job for up to a year afterwards. As our anecdotes have shown, all of this worked better in theory than in practice.

The big problem was that German regulation tied migration to many small conditions that needed to be met. In the case of entrepreneurs, they needed to prove that their business served an overriding economic interest or specific regional need, and that it would create positive spillovers for the economy. An entrepreneur was only exempted from this onerous process if they had seed capital of 1 million Deutschmarks and the expectation of creating at least ten jobs, after which the entrepreneur would still need to wait three years before obtaining permanent residence. This is similar to the US green-card system, apart from the US is a much more entrepreneur-friendly society and has no problems attracting high-skilled workers. The big problem with Germany is not so much getting in, but getting on.

In terms of what Kymlicka referred to as hardware,

Germany is not particularly restrictive if compared with other European countries. The UK's immigration regime is also restrictive, especially today, but life as a migrant in the UK is generally less discriminatory and they face fewer bureaucratic obstacles. Having lived in the UK, I have not experienced discrimination on the grounds that I originated from elsewhere.

There has been further liberalisation in Germany since. The Scholz government lengthened the job-search period for international students. It introduced the European Blue Card Directive for highly skilled labour, a special job-search visa for highly skilled and well-resourced individuals. It opened migration pathways for medium-skilled professions.

In June 2023, the German government passed the Skilled Labour Immigration Act, which aims to make it easier to attract trained skilled workers to Germany. The federal government's website says: 'Germany is becoming a modern immigration country'. The declaration of Germany as an *Einwanderungsland* – an immigration country – is significant. It is intended as a U-turn from the era of Kohl, who declared the exact opposite. Immigration is subject to a lot of double-barrelled constructions, like *Immigrationskultur*, or *Willkommenskultur*, which loosely translate to 'culture of immigration', or 'culture of welcoming'. The meaning of these words is imprecise. They carry lots of associations, often negative. They are ideally suited for scare stories. In that context, it is quite courageous for the Scholz administration formally to declare that Germany is an immigration country. This is not something that wins you votes.

This new law was intended to complement Germany's skilled-labour strategy, which aims to get more women and older people into the jobs market and simplify training and further education. The aim is to remove bureaucratic hurdles that make it difficult to live and work in Germany.

Germany is moving in the right direction. It offers improved training programmes, has introduced more work flexibility and more childcare facilities. After half a century of skilled-labour immigration, Germany is for the first time starting to behave like an actor in a competitive market. This is what acute labour shortages do.

But the pace of change is not fast enough to offset the problems caused by deindustrialisation and the global shifts that are currently taking place. Many areas of discrimination have not been addressed, like the university sector's chronic lack of competitiveness in attracting top researchers.

Of the new avenues into the German labour market that have been liberalised, the EU blue card offers the most tangible improvements. But again, the story looks different on paper than in reality. It allows university graduates from non-EU countries to work in Germany – or, indeed, anywhere else in the EU. Those in possession of the blue card have the right to settle in another EU country and work for another country without having to go through the hassle of restarting their work permit and residency procedure from scratch. For skilled immigration, the blue card is the single most important game changer because it is European, not national.

This is great for immigrants, but it is far from clear that Germany will be a net beneficiary of the system. While the work environment remains often hostile to foreign workers and the thrust of policy focuses on limiting the number of immigrants, skilled or unskilled, Germany will continue to face competition from countries that are more hospitable, especially to highly skilled labour. This includes countries in Northern Europe, in Eastern Europe and in smaller Western European countries, like Belgium, where it is no handicap if you are proficient in English only.

Germany's notoriously inadequate digital infrastructure is one of the issues raised by many highly qualified foreigners in Germany. Chapter 2 dealt with digital illiteracy in Germany, but this issue is also interwoven with immigration. One example is the German preference for cash and the poor card-payment infrastructure. This is especially a problem for new immigrants who are not yet fully set up with a bank account. Expats also complain that German authorities are poorly organised because of a lack of digital equipment and that it takes too long to get important issues resolved.

In the digital industries, we find a similar problem as we do in the universities: the salaries are often not competitive. The business magazine *WirtschaftsWoche* has also found that a lot of German IT professionals leave for higher-salaried positions abroad.

The wage moderation that used to be one of the cornerstones of the German neo-mercantilist model has turned out to be a problem for attracting economic migrants of all kinds.

Together with the bureaucratic hurdles, low wages make Germany uncompetitive in the high-skilled labour market. In fact, it may also be causing highly skilled Germans to leave the country. German doctors often find that they get higher salaries elsewhere – even in the UK's cash-strapped National Health Service.

German salaries are mostly in the middle of international rankings, but this is not where you want to be in a sellers' market when confronting a shortage of labour. The reaction from business to the blue card scheme has been muted. The main complaint is about bureaucratic hurdles.

The head of the Berlin Immigration Office was particularly blunt in her criticism: 'In order to spot the 0.1 per cent of immigrating skilled workers who may not have a genuine employment contract in their pocket or have committed a criminal offence, we subject 99.9 per cent of interested parties to a complex procedure, which means that these people sometimes don't hear from us for months or years.'

This is the reality on the ground, even after the reforms. She describes the bureaucratic procedure that was still in place at the beginning of 2024 as follows:

A foreigner who wants to work in Germany applies for a visa at the embassy, often after having waited months for an appointment. Depending on the circumstances of the case, the embassy involves the foreigners' bureau or the Federal Employment Agency (BA) or both. If they agree, the embassy issues a visa. (. . .) As a rule, however, this is only for six weeks (. . .) After the six weeks have elapsed, the person wishing to immigrate must then go back to the foreigners' bureau, which will formally check the same thing again. Then an electronic residence card is ordered from the federal printing company, which can take four to six weeks. And then the immigrant has to go to the immigration office again to have the card's online function activated.

This lived experience of immigrants differs so much from the general idea among German elites that there is a world out there trying to get in. When the leader of the Federal Democratic Party, Christian Lindner, visited a university in Ghana to promote Germany as a market for graduates, he asked a group of students to raise their hands if they could imagine migrating to work in Germany. No one responded. Maybe he was just unlucky. But even asking such a question tells us that there is a fundamental disconnect between how Germans perceive themselves and how others perceive Germany. Germany is an attractive and rich country. But is has a real problem in the global marketplace for skilled workers because it treats them like illegal immigrants.

As an immigrant myself, I can testify that the real experience of immigration is not described by laws, but by interactions with other people. The experience of immigrants in Germany is not great. When my family and I recently visited the German embassy to renew our passports, we witnessed how people were treated in the much longer queue for visa applications. The German authorities ask for an impossible number of documents, which people often find difficult to collect. It's not just the old passport and maybe a proof of residence. Whenever complications arise – like a name change after marriage, a divorce, children with different nationalities – the bureaucracy becomes overwhelming for many applicants. Not every applicant gets treated with respect when difficulties arise.

Amid all this gloom, there is good news as well. The blue card has been a moderate success: 83 per cent of highly qualified foreign workers with a blue card remain in the country after five years. This is according to a study by the Federal Statistical Office, which surveyed people who received their residence permit between 2012 and 2017.

But, of the students who travelled with a blue card, only 55 per cent were still in Germany after five years. Not so great.

The bad news is that the number of people who get the blue card is very small, by international standards. A total of 200,000 blue cards were issued in Germany in the nine years from 2012 to 2020. This works out at an average of a little more than 20,000 a year. This is a country with a working population of 46 million – and a shortage of some half a million workers. Compare to this to Canada, which issued 139,459 people with Canadian permanent-residency status through the federal high-skilled programme in 2022 alone. This status is comparable to that of the blue card. Canada's working population is only 20 million. Moving in the right direction is a start, but at its current rate of issuance, the blue card has no chance of contributing to a significant reduction in the skills gap.

In a global survey on expat life, Germany came last out of

fifty-two countries for two years in a row. Germany scored particularly badly in areas such as housing, digital infrastructure, language and administration. Among the expats surveyed, 30 per cent did not feel at home in Germany and had no social network, 50 per cent complained about the difficulty of making friends in Germany, and 33 per cent agreed that Germans were unfriendly to foreigners.

That's the reality of where are today. The generalised failure of Germany's immigration policy is reflected by the very large number of articles quoted on this subject, many of which are listed in the end notes. And this is only the tip of the iceberg. The problems are very serious. There are attempts to address them, but these attempts are up against a lot of resistance.

It takes decades to change cultural stereotypes and prejudices. Labour markets adjust, but prejudices do not disappear overnight. Or even within a decade. Skills shortages were already a problem twenty years ago, when the Schröder government introduced the first national green-card scheme. The regime has improved, essentially with the latest immigration law, but the real hurdles are further down the line: a Kafkaesque bureaucracy that traps applications in permanent procedures; outright racism in some cases; discrimination at work; and the natural disadvantage of German as a hard language to learn. A lot of skilled workers succeed in Germany despite these obstacles. But the problem is that Germany needs many more than it currently has. The prevailing German angst is the one expressed by Friedrich Merz, the opposition leader, who talks about 'immigration into the social system', as though high-skilled immigrants were motivated by the citizens' income or Germany's *Willkommenskultur*. This is bordering on the delusional. The global labour markets have turned: the state and the companies are the ones that should be joining the queue.

Epilogue: What to Do

When I started writing this book in 2023, the German industrial economy had already been on a declining trend for around five years. By then, it was already clear that this was not the usual cyclical downturn that produced chronically disappointing growth figures, but something more serious. The world economy started to recover in 2024. But, by the summer of that year, the situation in Germany had not yet improved. The forecasts suggest that the German economy will show a weak recovery in 2025. This is a plausible scenario. The hallmark of structural decline is not negative growth year in, year out. It does not mean that the economy will be trapped in a permanent recession. There will be no deserted towns with tumbleweed blowing through the streets. It means that the economy will continue to fluctuate around a lower average growth rate. Economies in decline will have good years like everybody else. So will Germany.

Germany's economic under-performance came as a

surprise to the many fanboys of the German economic model – those who eulogised German corporatism, a non-competitive banking system, the labour-market institutions and, in particular, the reliance on industry and exports for economic growth. It was a model that worked for a very long time. The policy failure was to double down on an old model when the external circumstances changed. This was a policy choice, not an oversight. Germany decided not to invest in the digital economy, but to focus on the cost competitiveness of its existing industries. It meant that, once the old model hit a crisis, there was not a new one ready to take over.

When rich economies decline, the signs are not immediately visible: people go out a bit less; they spend a bit less; they don't go on holiday as often; they drive their cars for longer before replacing them. Governments, too, start to save. After a few years, you see it in the form of potholes on streets or permanent road closures. A German motorway, to the south of Dortmund, a critical transport link between the north and the south, has been closed for several years after tests found a bridge in acute danger of collapse. Further tests revealed that all 60 bridges on that motorway will have to repaired. It will take years until this motorway will reopen. Another bridge, on one of Germany's busiest motorways near Cologne, is closed to lorries in 2016, a decision that caused massive traffic chaos. It was not until the beginning of 2024 that the first part of a new bridge was reopened. Crumbling infrastructure is a sign of decline. You also see it in a mobile-telephone infrastructure that leaves parts of the countryside uncovered. And no, there is no 5G anywhere.

But, most seriously, you see it in the politics. For twelve years, Angela Merkel's CDU, its Bavarian sister party, the CSU, and the Social Democrats governed together in what became known as a grand coalition, leaving the country without an effective opposition. When an economy starts to decline, people become unhappy and angry. If there is no opposition, they end up voting for extremist parties.

Germany was a relative latecomer to this trend. The far-right has been strong in France, Italy and the Netherlands for much longer. The pivotal moment for Germany came in 2015 when Angela Merkel opened the doors to Syrian refugees. This was the moment when the Alternative for Germany party emerged on the political scene in a big way. The AfD had been founded a few years earlier by a group of economics professors who opposed Germany's membership of the eurozone. They hated the euro, but they were pro-immigration. The refugee crisis led to an internal party takeover by the right that pushed the professors out. The AfD has since moved further to the right, and even counts some neo-Nazis among its supporters.

After Russia's invasion of Ukraine in 2022, the AfD opposed German weapons deliveries to Ukraine – a position that proved very popular in eastern Germany, an AfD stronghold. Another party started up in early 2024, on the left of the political spectrum – this one founded by Sahra Wagenknecht, who hails from eastern Germany. She used to be an iconic figure of the German left, but broke with the Left Party over its support for Ukraine. In June 2024, she staged a parliamentary walkout when Volodymyr Zelensky, the Ukrainian president, addressed the Bundestag. Together, the parties of the far left and the far right account for some 25 per cent of electoral support. This is what you get when all the centrist parties huddle together in government for too long, and when, at the same time, your economy becomes over-reliant on a dysfunctional model. In the UK of the 1970s, unhappiness also resulted in policy radicalisation, except the first-past-the-post electoral system forced this to occur within the established Conservative and Labour parties.

Against this backdrop, the unlikely victory by Olaf Scholz's SPD in the 2021 federal election, and the coalition he agreed with the Greens and the liberal-conservative FDP, was a hopeful sign. The new coalition started with a lot of goodwill, focusing on some of the themes I have written about in this book, like the chronic under-investment in both environmental and digital technologies. It promised a €450-billion investment programme. For the first time since I could remember, German politicians had earnest conversations about modernisation and digitalisation. The Greens got their way on the energy transition: the target for the exit from coal would be brought forward from 2038 to 2030. Everyone agreed that Germany badly needed more digital investment. Unfortunately, it was nobody's number-one priority.

For a brief moment, I thought Germany might just turn the corner. That did not happen. The tragedy of the coalition is that they got distracted.

The green transition is more or less on track, but the

economic benefits are vastly exaggerated. Germany will remain reliant on gas, which it no longer imports through pipelines from Russia, but in the form of liquid natural gas at world market prices. The modernisation part of the coalition deal never happened. I am not blaming the coalition for Germany's economic crisis. That criticism – from the right – always seemed unfair to me. As I have argued in this book, the deep causes of Germany's structural slump go back decades. The problem is that the coalition has given up on solving the problem.

The coalition has been doubling down on the old model. Christian Lindner's FDP talked a lot about young entrepreneurs during the 2021 election campaign, but it was his allegiance to Porsche and VW that ultimately informed his party's economic policies. The FDP became the voice of opposition against electric cars. When fiscal austerity struck in the coalition's later years, it was investment in modern technology that was sacrificed first. Investments that do not get made do not scream, and nor do they vote. In the end, this government has done the same thing as its predecessors – it has ended up feeding the beast.

Germany's old economic model relied on qualified labour, cheap energy, globalisation and technological leadership. All of these factors, which had worked so much in Germany's favour, flipped within a few years. It was the cheap energy from Russia that powered the model. Back in 2021, the year before the Russian invasion of Ukraine, the Greens pushed for the cancellation of Nord Stream 2, the second leg of the Baltic Sea gas pipeline that connected Germany to the Russian gas network. Annalena Baerbock, who later became foreign minister, and who had been the Greens' lead candidate for the 2021 elections, talked about a post-industrial Germany. Together with the FDP's ideas for a friendlier regime for start-up companies, Germany appeared to be on a good path. It would still take years until the old economy would be reformed, but at least a start would have been made. But the neo-mercantilism ended up kicking in again – because the coalition was not clear enough about the objectives, and because other stuff intruded, as always happens.

By January 2022, the Russians had started to mobilise their troops near the Ukrainian border. After the invasion, which started on 24 February, Scholz immediately reacted with a stop on Nord Stream 2. He had coordinated his position closely with President Joe Biden, the only foreign leader with whom Scholz would ever build a close relationship. As part of the deal, the US would become the biggest provider of financial and military support for Ukraine, while the Germans would kill Nord Stream 2 and lead the European efforts to help Ukraine. Scholz, however, initially prevailed with his insistence on keeping the Russian gas flowing through the existing pipeline, Nord Stream 1.

Scholz was the resident transatlanticist in his party, but he was still a fully paid-up subscriber to the German corporatist model. His foreign-policy adviser, Jens Plöttner, was part of the pro-Russian consensus among Social Democrats. Even that autumn, more than six months after Putin's invasion,

Plöttner was still peddling the line that the most interesting question about the war was not what would happen to Ukraine, but how the relationship between Russia and Germany would evolve after the war. Germany always wanted everything – a transatlantic alliance to protect its security, an EU internal market, and special relations with Russia and China. It took the German policy establishment a long time to realise that this was no longer possible.

After the invasion of Ukraine, the war became the main focus of policy. The project of renewal had to wait. In March, shortly after Putin's invasion, Scholz gave a remarkable speech in the Bundestag in which he announced what he called an 'epochal change' – a shift in Germany's defence and security policies. The government would increase defence spending to 2 per cent of GDP, which Merkel had committed to but in which she and her coalitions had never invested any political capital. Scholz's own U-turn on this point was cemented by an announcement that the war in Ukraine would justify a €100-billion fund for investments in the *Bundeswehr* (German armed forces). Together with the ordinary defence budget, the combined annual defence spending would immediately meet the NATO target – but only for a few years. Outside of Germany, his speech was widely noted and unfortunately over-interpreted by the defence and foreign-policy community. It gave the impression that Germany was changing, when in reality it was trying so save what was left of the old model.

Those who fell for the 'epochal change' smoke-and-mirrors

trick didn't know Scholz. And they didn't know the dynamics of German politics. Very soon, this joint modernisation project was unravelling. It did not happen in a Big Bang, but came in small discrete steps, very much like the unravelling of the economic model itself.

In September 2022, the Nord Stream 2 pipelines were blown up. That ended Scholz's delusion that Germany could continue relying on Russian gas while supporting Ukraine in the war. Around the same time, the coalition had its first big disagreement, over the future of the three remaining nuclear power stations, which were due to go offline by the end of 2022. Robert Habeck, the Greens' economics minister, insisted that the coalition should stick to the agreed timetable. Nuclear power had a totemic quality for the Greens, as we have seen, since the party's very existence had sprung from anti-nuclear protest movements. Now, they were in charge of the economics ministry for the first time ever; there was no way they would let go of capturing the big prize – the decommissioning of the final six power stations.

The first three came offline on schedule, a few weeks after the new government had been formed, in January 2022. Then came Putin's invasion and the rise in energy prices. Pressure for a delay in the phasing-out of the final three power stations increased. The FDP in particular wanted to keep them online for the foreseeable future. Scholz intervened in the dispute and sided with Habeck and the Greens, but gave the FDP a fig leaf. He decreed that the final power stations would come offline three months later than scheduled, in April 2023. He justified the delay as an insurance against a cold winter. The winter turned out to be warm. In April 2023, the three reactors came offline as scheduled. This was the end of nuclear power in Germany. It will never come back.

In 2023, the pandemic was mostly behind us, and the war in Ukraine fell off the front pages of the newspapers. In the summer of 2023, Habeck launched the biggest green project of this legislature. The domestic heating bill was a law to force households to change their heating systems from gas and oil heaters to expensive electric heat pumps. The original draft had 2024 as the cut-off for all new installations. By 2030, all old systems would have to be replaced. For many homeowners, especially for those living in poorer neighbourhoods, the cost of the change would be out of all proportion to the value of their homes. The domestic heating bill was a disaster for the government, and for the Greens in particular. House prices started falling as a result. The heating bill was later watered down, but the political damage persisted. The governing partners had squabbled before, but it was the heating-bill controversy that revealed the deep fissures running through this coalition. It was the beginning of the anti-green backlash.

Shortly after the heating-bill controversy came the final blow: the German constitutional court ruled that the government had misspent funds set aside for the COVID pandemic by funnelling them into the climate budget. This ruling took between €50 billion and €60 billion out of German public spending, most of it in the 2024 and 2025 budgets. No government can recover from such a fiscal shock, especially not a fractious coalition that disagrees on economic policy. I have never seen a Western European government impose an austerity programme of that size in such a short space of time – and live beyond the next election day.

I personally have no sympathy for them. The SPD was the co-inventor of the debt brake. When they came to power, they suffered buyer's remorse. No single event has contributed to the political misfortune of this coalition more than the constitutional court's ruling against the coalition's budget policies. I am not blaming the court. The ruling has a legal logic that is hard to dispute. It is not the role of a court to impose good economic policies on governments. The government knew it was taking a risk when it diverted unspent COVID money to the climate fund. This is what bad policy rules do: they give rise to more bad policies to circumvent the initial ones. When successive governments get caught up in these games, and focus on meeting silly technical targets, they lose sight of the big picture. This is what happened here. Everybody lost their sense of strategic directive.

When they got elected, the coalition partners managed to overcome their differences through money. Everybody got what they wanted. The SPD got their minimum wage, a universal citizens' income and pension reform. The Greens got the climate transition. And the FDP was able to protect the car industry against a motorway speed limit. Lindner himself got the big prize: the finance ministry. Once the court took the money away, the political differences between the parties came out in the open.

In early 2024, the tension between the coalition partners had reached boiling point. The Greens and the FDP were the main adversaries. But personal tensions also started to rise between Lindner and Scholz. By the early summer of 2024, the green modernisation project had lost much political support. The main result of the European elections was an anti-green backlash. The Green Agenda, which Ursula von der Leyen compared to Europe's man-on-the-moon moment in 2019, faced an uncertain future. Germany was experiencing a conflict between conservative rural communities and left-leaning metropolitan areas. It was the first time I heard Germans complain about the 'metropolitian elite' – something I had only heard in the UK and the US previously. The backlash against the Greens, in Germany and in Europe, was well under way.

The political counterpart to the decline of the Greens was the rise in support for the far right. Between the summer of 2023 and the spring of 2024, the right-wing Alternative for Germany enjoyed an explosive rise in its poll ratings, to 23 per cent. In early 2024, Sahra Wagenknecht, who had split away from the Left Party a year earlier, started her own party, BSW, and immediately got 6.2 per cent at the European election. BSW is a party of the left with themes of the right. Wagenknecht opposes immigration, and Germany's support for Ukraine. When President Volodymyr Zelenski of

Ukraine visited the Bundestag in June 2024, Wagenknecht and her party members walked out.

The AfD, beset by scandals, did not get as much as its poll ratings earlier in the year suggested. What has remained stable is the sum-total of support for radical parties – parties that oppose the renewal of the economy. Both Wagenknecht and AfD want to reopen the gas pipelines and revert to the strategic partnership with Russia and China. They want out of NATO. The AfD wants to quit the EU. Wagenknecht wants Germany to stay in the EU, but wants to oppose all of its legislation and, if passed, not implement any new laws. These two parties represent approximately a quarter of the electorates. And it is not as though the other three-quarters agree on what to do.

The political landscape has become too fractured to enact the reforms needed for Germany to end the structural slump. Germany is not alone here. Other European countries suffer the same problem. I wrote at the beginning of the book that this is a narrative of what happened, not a policy book. If there is one single measure I may suggest, it would be a European capital-markets union – the full-monty version, with a single sovereign asset. The objective would be to break the toxic nexus between banks and their home governments, and between banks and old industry. Public-sector investment is important. It is the lack of capital flows to most profitable businesses that hampers Europe's economic development.

Such a reform is hard to imagine, especially now that the

hard right is on the march in many European countries. The tragedy is that, during the grand-coalition years under Merkel, Germany had the political majorities to reform the system. This is going to become progressively harder. The rise of the extreme parties is the ultimate throwback to the bad old days of industrial corporatism, when German chancellors and Russian presidents would strike deals, and when German company chiefs would travel to the St Petersburg International Economic Forum.

Modern Germany has never known anything other than corporatist industrial society. There is a degree of managed friendly conflict between trade unions and employers, but both ultimately operate within the same system. On the big questions, they agree. Successive governments have regarded it as a priority of German foreign policy to help German companies secure orders and to support the interests of domestic industry at home, in Brussels and abroad.

Olaf Scholz and his government did not see this crisis coming. Even the Greens were fully paid-up subscribers to the corporatist industrial model. For all their political differences, they all agreed on this. Industry was good. The right wanted industrial profits. The left wanted industrial jobs. The Greens dreamt of a green industry. Nobody questioned the over-reliance on industry itself. Instead of diversifying away from traditional industry towards other sectors, Germany doubled down.

It was the only system they ever knew.

Notes

PROLOGUE

Po Yin Wong and Mohammad Amin, 'Should we be thinking more about imports?', Worldbank.org, 12 June 2014, https://blogs.worldbank.org/en/developmenttalk/should-we-be-thinking-more-about-imports

Wikipedia Contributors, 'High-definition television', Wikipedia, accessed 1 April 2024, https://en.wikipedia.org/wiki/High-definition_television

'Neues Börsensegment: Nie wieder Neuer Markt', *Tagesspiegel*, 21 November 2016, https://www.tagesspiegel.de/wirtschaft/nie-wieder-neuer-markt-3775462.html

Mathias Müller von Blumencron, 'Ein Besuch beim Aldi-Gründer: Karl Albrecht: "Ich habe Glück gehabt"', *Frankfurter Allgemeine Zeitung*, 21 July 2014, https://www.faz.net/aktuell/wirtschaft/menschen-wirtschaft/ein-besuch-bei-aldi-gruender-karl-albrecht-13057122.html?printPagedArticle=true#pageIndex_2

'Nobel Prize Laureates from Göttingen: The Göttingen Nobel Prize Wonder', Georg-August-Universität Göttingen (press release), 2014, https://www.uni-goettingen.de/en/nobel+prize+laureates+from+göttingen/4281.html

Hermann Simon, 'Lessons from Germany's Midsize Giants', *Harvard Business Review*, March–April 1992, https://hbr.org/1992/03/lessons-from-germanys-midsize-giants

Nicholas Negroponte, *Being Digital* (London: Hodder & Stoughton, 1995).

CHAPTER I: THE CANARY

T. Andresen, 'Drei-Säulen-Struktur: Umbruch: Vom Verschwinden der Banken', *Handelsblatt*, 2009, handelsblatt.de.

Beat Balzli, Christoph Pauly and Wolfgang Reuter, 'Germany's Latest Banking Crisis: Will Savings Banks Be the Next Casualties?', *Der Spiegel*, 27 May 2009, https://www.spiegel.de/international/business/germany-s-latest-banking-crisis-will-savings-banks-be-the-next-casualties-a-627153.html

Stefan Berg, Georg Bönisch, Thomas Darnstädt and Barbara Schmid, 'Die rote Kasse der Genossen', *Der Spiegel*, 13 February 2000, https://www.spiegel.de/politik/die-rote-kasse-der-genossen-a-6a6c5 2d9-0002-0001-0000-000015680633

Michael Berlemann and Vera Jahn, 'Ist der deutsche Mittelstand tatsächlich ein Innovationsmotor?', *ifo Schnelldienst* 67, no. 17, 2014, pp. 22–8, https://www.ifo.de/publikationen/2014/aufsatz-zeitschrift/ist-der-deutsche-mittelstand-tatsaechlich-ein

Georg Bönisch, Barbara Schmid and Andrea Stuppe, 'Stumpfe Sichel', *Der Spiegel*, 2 April 2000, https://www.spiegel.de/politik/stumpfe-sichel-a-a121e371-0002-0001-0000-000016098319

Thilo Boss, 'Zerstört die EU Ihr Lebenswerk, Herr Neuber?' *Die Welt*, 19 November 2000, https://www.welt.de/print-welt/article548083/Zerstoert-die-EU-Ihr-Lebenswerk-Herr-Neuber.html

Christian Rusche, 'Deindustrialisierung: Eine Analyse auf Basis von Direktinvestitionen', *IW-Kurzbericht*, no. 43, 28 June 2023, https://www.iwkoeln.de/studien/christian-rusche-eine-analyse-auf-basis-von-direktinvestitionen.html

'Eine feindliche Übernahme', *Der Spiegel*, 13 October 1991, https://www.spiegel.de/wirtschaft/eine-feindliche-uebernahme-a-daf50725-0002-0001-0000-000013491523

Klaus P. Weinert, 'Tradition versus Moderne?', Deutschlandfunk (website), 14 January 2001, https://www.deutschlandfunk.de/tradition-versus-moderne-102.html

Deutsche Presse-Agentur, 'Deutscher Bankentag: Privatbanken fordern Aufbrechen des Kreditmarktes', *Handelsblatt*, 25 April 2006, https://www.handelsblatt.com/finanzen/banken-versicherungen/banken/deutscher-bankentag-privatbanken-fordern-aufbrechen-des-kreditmarktes/2645450.html

'Insolvenz: Rettungsversuch für Babcock-Borsig gescheitert', *Frankfurter Allgemeine Zeitung*, 8 July 2002, https://www.faz.net/aktuell/politik/insolvenz-rettungsversuch-fuer-babcock-borsig-gescheitert-171070.html

'Landesbanken: Das Drama der Landesbanken', FinanzWende (website), 6 December 2019, https://www.finanzwende.de/themen/banken-und-schattenbanken/landesbanken/

Max Flötotto, Philipp Koch, Reinhard Höll, Peter Laaber, Elena Moschner, Carolin Brückmann and Brigit Teschke, 'Deutschlands Banken zurück im Spiel', McKinsey & Co., 19 July 2021, https://www.mckinsey.de/publikationen/german-banking-report

Hans-Hermann Francke and Michael Hudson, *Banking and Finance in West Germany* (RLE Banking and Finance), (Abingdon and New York: Routledge, 1984).

Guillaume Gilquin, 'Der deutsche Bankensektor', *Wirtschaftsdienst* 94, 2014(6), pp. 420–7, https://www.wirtschaftsdienst.eu/inhalt/jahr/2014/heft/6/beitrag/der-deutsche-bankensektor.html

'Porträt: Friedel Neuber war der mächtigste Staatsbanker Deutschlands', *Handelsblatt*, 2004, handelsblatt.de. https://www.handelsblatt.com/archiv/portraet-friedel-neuber-war-der-maechtigste-staatsbanker-deutschlands/2423118.html

'Christian Sewing: Deutsche-Bank-Chef entschuldigt sich offenbar bei Finanzministerium und Bafin für Analysten-Kritik', *Handelsblatt*, 17 September 2021, https://www.handelsblatt.com/finanzen/banken-versicherungen/banken/christian-sewing-deutsche-bank-chef-entschuldigt-sich-offenbar-bei-finanzministerium-und-bafin-fuer-analysten-kritik/27623022.html

Harald Hau and Marcel Thum, 'Subprime crisis and board (in-)competence: private versus public banks in Germany', *Economic Policy* 24(60), 1 October 2009, pp. 701–52, https://doi.org/10.1111/j.1468-0327.2009.00232.x

Christine Heuer, Uschi Götz and Michael Braun, 'Geldgeschäfte in Politikerhand', Deutschlandfunk (website), 23 October 2008, https://www.deutschlandfunk.de/geldgeschaefte-in-politikerhand-100.html

IMF, *Germany's Three-Pillar Banking System: Cross-Country Perspectives in Europe*, (Washington, DC: International Monetary Fund, 21 June 2004), https://www.elibrary.imf.org/display/book/9781589063488/9781589063488.xml

NOTES

IMF, 'Germany: Technical Note on Banking Sector Structure', *IMF Staff Country Reports*, Volume 2011, Issue 370, 23 December 2011, https://www.elibrary.imf.org/view/journals/002/2011/370/002.2011.issue-370-en.xml

Sönke Iwersen and Volker Votsmeier, 'Cum-Ex-Skandal: Hamburg als Paradies für Steuersünder', *Handelsblatt*, 26 August 2023, https://www.handelsblatt.com/finanzen/banken-versicherungen/cum-ex/cum-ex-skandal-hamburg-als-paradies-fuer-steuersuender/29343810.html

Thomas Jesch, *Die Fördergeld-Strategie 2021: Fördergelder akquirieren für Existenzgründer sowie kleine und mittlere Unternehmen*, (Munich: FinanzBuch Verlag, 2021).

Gunter Kayser, 'Mittelstandsfinanzierung in der Bundesrepublik Deutschland [...]', Yumpu (website), n.d. (retrieved 3 July 2023), https://www.yumpu.com/de/document/read/6171489/mittelstandsfinanzierung-in-der-bundesrepublik-deutschland-

Andreas Kröner, 'Finanzsektor: Commerzbank-Chef attackiert Sparkassen und Volksbanken', *Handelsblatt*, 21 September 2021, https://www.handelsblatt.com/finanzen/banken-versicherungen/banken/finanzsektor-commerzbank-chef-attackiert-sparkassen-und-volksbanken/27632294.html

Anne Kunz, 'CDU und CSU haben großen Einfluss auf die Sparkassen', *Die Welt*, 17 June 2018, https://www.welt.de/wirtschaft/article177676252/Parteien-haben-grossen-Einfluss-auf-die-Sparkassen.html

Rafael La Porta, Florencio Lopez-De-Silanes and Andrei Shleifer, 'Government Ownership of Banks', *The Journal of Finance*, 57(1), February 2002, pp. 265–301, https://doi.org/10.1111/1540-6261.00422

'Holzmann: Sanierungs-Tarifvertrag gescheitert', *Manager Magazin*, 29 February 2000, https://www.manager-magazin.de/finanzen/artikel/a-67175.html

Yasmin Osman, 'Deutsche Bank: Ex-Chef Josef Ackermann teilt aus', *Handelsblatt*, 5 July 2023, https://www.handelsblatt.com/finanzen/banken-versicherungen/banken/deutsche-bank-ex-chef-josef-ackermann-teilt-aus/29236746.html

Christoph Rottwilm, 'Sechs Monate nach der Scheidung: So lebt der Dax ohne Linde – und so Linde ohne den Dax', *Manager Magazin*, 28 August 2023, https://www.manager-magazin.de/finanzen/geldanlage/linde-und-dax-so-lebt-der-dax-ohne-linde-und-so-linde-ohne-den-dax-a-b1cd9362-b3ec-4a43-acec-233d83ee2d06

Christoph Scherrer, 'Öffentliche Banken bedürfen gesellschaftlicher Aufsicht', *Kurswechsel*, 4/2014, pp. 16–24.

Jan Schildbach, 'Reformagenda für den Finanzplatz Deutschland', Deutsche Bank Research, 14 September 2021, https://sven-giegold. de/wp-content/uploads/2021/09/Reformagenda_fu%CC%88r_den_ Finanzplatz_Deutschland_DB.pdf

Daniel Seikel, *Der Kampf um öffentlich-rechtliche Banken: Wie die Europäische Kommission Liberalisierung durchsetzt*, (Frankfurt: Campus Verlag, 2013).

Daniel Seikel, 'Savings banks and Landesbanken in the German political economy: The long struggle between private and public banks', in Christoph Scherrer (ed.), *Public Banks int eh Age of Financialization*, (Cheltenham: Edward Elgar Publishing, 2017), pp. 155–175, https://doi. org/10.4337/9781786430663.00020

Bankengruppen—Marktanteile an Bilanzsumme der deutschen Bankenbranche 2022', Statista (website), September 2022, https:// de.statista.com/statistik/daten/studie/166006/umfrage/marktanteile- der-bankengruppen-in-deutschland/

Christine Trampusch, Benedikt Linden and Michael Schwan, 'Staatskapitalismus in NRW und Bayern: Der Aufstieg und Fall von WestLB und BayernLB', *Zeitschrift Für Vergleichende Politikwissenschaft* 8, 2014, pp. 129–54, https://doi.org/10.1007/s12286-014-0201-1

CHAPTER 2: NEULAND

Laura Stresing, 'Die Bundesregierung setzt auf veraltete Konzepte', t-online (website), 7 March 2019, https://www.t-online.de/digital/ aktuelles/id_85279884/kuenstliche-intelligenz-die-ki-strategie-der- bundesregierung-setzt-auf-veraltete-konzepte-.html

Sven Astheimer and Stephan Finsterbusch, 'Kernfusion-Pionier Marvel: "Kein einziges Angebot in Europa"', *Frankfurter Allgemeine Zeitung*, 7 August 2023, https://www.faz.net/aktuell/wirtschaft/unternehmen/ marvel-fusion-warum-das-start-up-aus-muenchen-in-die-usa- zieht-19084658.html

Notker Blechner, 'Hintergrund: Absatzmarkt Asien: Schicksal der Autobauer hängt an China', Tagesschau (website), 28 July 2022, https:// www.tagesschau.de/wirtschaft/unternehmen/china-autobauer-vw- mercedes-bmw-byd-eletroautos-uiguren-101.html

Bundesministerium für Wirtschaft und Klimaschutz (Federal Ministry for Economic Affairs and Climate Protection), 'Automobilindustrie', BMWK (website), 29 February 2020, https://www.bmwk.de/Redaktion/DE/Textsammlungen/Branchenfokus/Industrie/branchenfokus-automobilindustrie.html

'So verteidigt die Bundesregierung ihre KI-Strategie', t-online (website), 7 March 2019, https://www.t-online.de/digital/aktuelles/id_85366378/kuenstliche-intelligenz-ohne-deep-learning-bundesregierung-verteidigt-ihre-ki-strategie.html

'Intel-Chipfabrik in Magdeburg: Zukunftsinvestitionen gegen Staatsknete', Deutschlandfunk (website), 27 June 2023, https://www.deutschlandfunk.de/intel-fabrik-chips-subventionen-magdeburg-100.html

'Schule: Lehrerverband warnt vor "totaler Zwangsdigitalisierung"', Deutschlandfunk Kultur (website), https://www.deutschlandfunkkultur.de/schule-lehrerverband-warnt-vor-totaler-zwangsdigitalisierung-100.html

Deutsche Presse-Agentur, 'Lobbyismus: FDP weist Porschegate-Vorwürfe zurück', Die Zeit, 23 July 2022, https://www.zeit.de/news/2022-07/23/fdp-weist-porschegate-vorwuerfe-zurueck

Alexander Eydlin, Deutsche Presse-Agentur and Agence France-Presse, 'Digitalisierung an Schulen: Deutschland liegt bei digitaler Schulausstattung international zurück', 29 September 2020, Die Zeit, https://www.zeit.de/gesellschaft/schule/2020-09/digitalisierung-schulen-schlechte-ausstattung-deutschland-osze-internationaler-vergleich

Michael Freitag and Claas Tatje, 'Der Masterplan des Aufsichtsratschefs: New Conti – wie der Autozulieferer neu aufgestellt werden soll', Manager Magazin, 22 August 2023, https://www.manager-magazin.de/unternehmen/autoindustrie/continental-aufsichtsrat-bereitet-aufspaltung-vor-autosparte-koennte-verkauft-werden-a-2ed038b6-97c4-428d-a6f9-0f426ce65b3d

G. Hamann and D. H. Lamparter, 'Martin Winterkorn: "Mir geht's gut"', Die Zeit, https://www.zeit.de/2013/10/Volkswagen-Chef-Martin-Winterkorn/seite-3

'Aufbruch in eine neue Zeit – das große Handelsblatt-KI-Special', Handelsblatt, 30 June 2023, https://www.handelsblatt.com/downloads/29231622/16/ki-sonderausgabe.pdf

Philipp Alvares de Souza Soares, 'Kommentar: Faesers Kritik an der Telekom im Streit um Huawei-Technik ist bigott', *Handelsblatt*, 18 August 2023, https://www.handelsblatt.com/meinung/kommentare/kommentar-faesers-kritik-an-der-telekom-im-streit-um-huawei-technik-ist-bigott/29339890.html

Markus Fasse and Martin Murphy, 'Warum Mercedes – und BMW – Manager bei VW so oft scheitern', *Handelsblatt*, 19 July 2023, https://www.handelsblatt.com/karriere/diess-duesmann-warum-mercedes-und-bmw-manager-bei-vw-so-oft-scheitern/29245550.html

'Autoindustrie: Mercedes sieht "dramatischen Preiskampf" bei E-Autos in China', *Handelsblatt*, 13 July 2023, https://www.handelsblatt.com/unternehmen/industrie/autoindustrie-mercedes-sieht-dramatischen-preiskampf-bei-e-autos-in-china/29258304.html

Felix Holtermann, 'Künstliche Intelligenz: Warum die USA den Europäern bei KI-Investments den Rang ablaufen', *Handelsblatt*, 12 July 2023, https://www.handelsblatt.com/technik/ki/kuenstliche-intelligenz-warum-die-usa-den-europaeern-bei-ki-investments-den-rang-ablaufen/29247542.html

Lisa Hegemann, 'Digitalisierung: Wenn Politik auf künstliche Intelligenz trifft', *Die Zeit*, 15 November 2018, https://www.zeit.de/digital/internet/2018-11/digitalisierung-ki-strategie-investitionen-bundesregierung/komplettansicht

Sepp Hochreiter, 'The Vanishing Gradient Problem During Learning Recurrent Neural Nets and Problem Solutions', *International Journal of Uncertainty Fuzziness and Knowledge-Based Systems*, 6(2), April 1998, pp. 107–16, https://www.researchgate.net/publication/220355039_The_Vanishing_Gradient_Problem_During_Learning_Recurrent_Neural_Nets_and_Problem_Solutions

'Where Ford will slash jobs in Europe', *Automotive News Europe*, 23 January 2023, https://europe.autonews.com/automakers/where-ford-will-slash-jobs-europe

Jakob von Lindern, 'Digitalisierung an Schulen: Die Milliarden, die nicht ankommen', *Die Zeit*, 26 January 2021, https://www.zeit.de/digital/2021-01/digitalpakt-schule-fernunterricht-homeschooling-tablets-foederalismus-digitale-bildung

Michael Kerler, 'Interview: "Deutsche Hersteller haben das Elektroauto verschlafen"', *Augsburger Allgemeine*, 26 January 2017, https://www.augsburger-allgemeine.de/wirtschaft/Interview-Deutsche-Hersteller-haben-das-Elektroauto-verschlafen-id40314177.html

Eva Müller, 'Digitale Infrastruktur: Deutschlands Internet wird zum Standort-Risiko', *Manager Magazin*, 12 May 2014, https://www.manager-magazin.de/magazin/artikel/a-963827.html

'Emden: VW drosselt Produktion von E-Autos und streicht Schicht', NDR (website), 26 June 2023, https://www.ndr.de/nachrichten/niedersachsen/oldenburg_ostfriesland/Emden-VW-drosselt-Produktion-von-E-Autos-und-streicht-Schicht,vw5996.html

Sebastian Schaal, 'Elektroautos Deutscher Hersteller: Eine Geschichte der verpassten Chancen', *WirtschaftsWoche*, 1 October 2017, https://www.wiwo.de/unternehmen/auto/elektroautos-deutscher-hersteller-eine-geschichte-der-verpassten-chancen/20391252-all.html

'Top-Ökonomen kritisieren Intel-Subvention scharf', Tagesschau (website), 19 June 2023, https://www.tagesschau.de/wirtschaft/unternehmen/intel-foederung-subvention-kritik-oekonomen-100.html

'Offener Brief: Mobilitätsgipfel statt Autogipfel', LobbyControl (website), 7 September 2020, https://www.lobbycontrol.de/lobbyismus-und-klima/offener-brief-mobilitaetsgipfel-statt-autogipfel-81603/

Victoria Waldersee, Jan Schwartz and Tom Sims, 'VW's CEO Diess ousted after tumultuous tenure, Porsche's Blume to succeed', Reuters, 22 July 2022, https://www.reuters.com/business/autos-transportation/volkswagens-ceo-diess-leave-company-2022-07-22/

ZDFheute Nachrichten, 'E-Mobilität: China hängt Deutsche Autobauer ab – was dahintersteckt | auslandsjournal', 2023, YouTube video, https://www.youtube.com/watch?v=A1genk-grpQ&ab_channel=ZDFheuteNachrichten

Jürgen Berke, 'Langsames Internet: Ist dieser Mann an allem schuld?', *WirtschaftsWoche*, 24 January 2018, https://www.wiwo.de/politik/deutschland/langsames-internet-ist-dieser-mann-an-allem-schuld/20859440.html

Ruth Ciesinger, 'Schule und Digitalisierung: Wie Schulen sich für die digitale Zukunft ändern müssen', *Tagesspiegel*, 12 April 2018, https://www.tagesspiegel.de/politik/wie-schulen-sich-fur-die-digitale-zukunft-andern-mussen-8422819.html

Stephan Finsterbusch and Uwe Marx, 'Hannover Messe: "Ich mache mir Sorgen um den Standort Deutschland"', *Frankfurter Allgemeine Zeitung*, 20 April 2024, https://www.faz.net/aktuell/wirtschaft/unternehmen/vdma-praesident-haeusgen-und-zwei-chef-kegel-ueber-die-hannover-messe-2024-19663704.html

Ulf Sommer, Christoph Herwartz, „Forschung und Entwicklung: US-Konzerne bauen ihren Vorsprung aus" *Handelsblatt*, 4 May 2023 https://www.handelsblatt.com/unternehmen/management/die-forschungsintensivsten-unternehmen-der-welt-forschung-und-entwicklung-us-konzerne-bauen-ihren-vorsprung-aus/29125786.html

Axel Höpner and Sebastian Matthes, 'Roland Busch im Interview: "Europa ist groß genug für eine eigene Chipindustrie"', *Handelsblatt*, 14 July 2023, https://www.handelsblatt.com/unternehmen/industrie/roland-busch-im-interview-europa-ist-gross-genug-fuer-eine-eigene-chipindustrie/29256110.html

Kathrin Witsch, Euopaeische Greentechs gehen verstaerkt in die USA', *Handelsblatt*, 7 Apr 2023, , https://www.handelsblatt.com/unternehmen/energie/marvel-fusion-europaeische-greentechs-gehen-verstaerkt-in-die-usa/29279030.html

Pelle Kohrs, 'Für Kinder erklärt: Warum das Internet in Deutschland so langsam ist', *Dein Spiegel*, 7 May 2021, https://www.spiegel.de/deinspiegel/breitbandausbau-warum-das-internet-in-deutschland-so-langsam-ist-a-4ae2e73a-0002-0001-0000-000176028069

Martin Noé, 'Innovationshindernis Staat: Wie Schlummerland eine Fabrik für Vertical Farming ausbremst', *Manager Magazin*, 1 August 2023, https://www.manager-magazin.de/unternehmen/landwirtschaft-wie-die-buerokratie-vertical-farming-ausbremst-ein-fallbeispiel-aus-brandenburg-a-2226f17c-8e45-4a62-b970-5f3958dda73b

Marcel Rosenbach and Hilmar Schmundt, 'Deutschlands Schwächen bei künstlicher Intelligenz: »Lasst die Leute rein!«', *Der Spiegel*, 20 December 2022, https://www.spiegel.de/wissenschaft/technik/kuenstliche-intelligenz-in-deutschland-die-deutsche-ki-strategie-befindet-sich-im-blindflug-a-d49d0051-4d8a-4b7e-a944-79f584e24760

'Sauerland: Pferd bei Experiment schneller als Daten-Übertragung per Internet', *Rheinische Post*, 21 December 2020, https://rp-online.de/nrw/panorama/sauerland-pferd-bei-experiment-schneller-als-daten-uebertragung-per-internet_aid-55326413

Stefan Schaible and David Born, 'Deutschland bleibt innovativ, aber es fehlt der Schwung', Roland Berger (website), 3 May 2023, https://www.rolandberger.com/de/Insights/Publications/Deutschland-bleibt-innovativ-aber-es-fehlt-der-Schwung.html

Christian Stöcker, 'Webzugänge: Merkel verspricht High-Speed-Internet für Millionen Deutsche', *Der Spiegel*, 28 February 2009, https://www.

spiegel.de/netzwelt/tech/webzugaenge-merkel-verspricht-high-speed-
internet-fuer-millionen-deutsche-a-610503.html

'Neue PISA-Studie: Deutsche Schüler schneiden so schlecht ab wie nie',
Tagesschau (website), 5 December 2023, https://www.tagesschau.de/
inland/gesellschaft/pisa-studie-128.html

Mariana Mazzucato and Travis Whitfill, 'Expanding DARPA's model of
innovation for biopharma: A proposed Advanced Research Projects
Agency for Health', UCL Institute for Innovation and Public Purpose,
Working Paper Series (IIPP WP 2020-09), 24 June 2022, https://www.
ucl.ac.uk/bartlett/public-purpose/publications/2022/jun/expanding-
darpas-model-innovation-biopharma

Kate Whiting, 'Germany is the world's most innovative economy', World
Economic Forum (website), 18 October 2018, https://www.weforum.
org/agenda/2018/10/germany-is-the-worlds-most-innovative-economy/

Florian Zandt, 'Infografik: Im dritten Gang über die Datenautobahn',
Statista (website), 22 March 2022, https://de.statista.com/
infografik/27083/anteil-der-breitbandanschluesse-in-deutschland-die-
mindestens-folgende-eebertragungsraten-erreicht-haben/

Volker Zimmermann, 'Die Finanzierung von Digitalisierung und
Investitionen in mittelständischen Unternehmen im Vergleich', KfW
Research, 9 March 2020, https://www.dg-medienportal.de/bi_wp/wp-
content/uploads/PDF/Nachrichten/2020/Fokus-Nr.-280-Maerz-2020-
Finanzierung-Digitalisierung-1.pdf

CHAPTER 3: FRIENDS OF GERHARD

'Gabriel, Steinmeier und die Geheimakte Nord Stream',
abgeordnetenwatch.de (website), 5 February 2023, https://www.
abgeordnetenwatch.de/newsletter/gabriel-steinmeier-und-die-
geheimakte-nord-stream

Oliver Bilger, 'Deutschland – Russland: Eine vergiftete Freundschaft',
Handelsblatt, 16 November 2012, https://www.handelsblatt.com/
politik/international/deutschland-russland-eine-vergiftete-
freundschaft/7398250.html

Reinhard Bingener and Markus Wehner, *Die Moskau Connection: Das
Schröder-Netzwerk und Deutschlands Weg in die Abhängigkeit*, (Munich:
C. H. Beck, 2023).

Daniel Brössler, '70 Jahre Ost-Ausschuss: Moskaus bester Ex-Partner', *Süddeutsche Zeitung*, 12 December 2022, https://www.sueddeutsche.de/wirtschaft/ost-ausschuss-moskau-ukraine-70-jahre-1.5714146

Jan Dams, Carsten Dierig, Martin Greive and Eduard Steiner, 'Investitionsboom: So tricksen sich deutsche Konzerne nach Russland', *Die Welt*, 2 July 2016, https://www.welt.de/wirtschaft/article156565666/So-tricksen-sich-deutsche-Konzerne-nach-Russland.html

'Siemens-Chef verteidigt Geschäfte mit Russland', *Der Spiegel*, 27 March 2014, https://www.spiegel.de/wirtschaft/unternehmen/siemens-joe-kaeser-verteidigt-geschaefte-mit-putin-und-russland-a-961005.html

"Wir haben ein Problem": Gewerkschaft warnt vor Folgen bei Verzicht auf russisches Gas', *RND*, 25 January 2022, https://www.rnd.de/politik/nord-stream-2-gewerkschaft-warnt-vor-verzicht-auf-russisches-gas-NXPXEA6OPA3D2MT7FXNHJMJGDE.html

'Maschinenbauer: Mit Samthandschuhen nach Russland', *Handelsblatt*, 8 August 2015, https://www.handelsblatt.com/unternehmen/industrie/maschinenbauer-mit-samthandschuhen-nach-russland/12147928.html

Monika Dunkel and Timo Pache, 'Interview: "Wir müssen Putin zeigen, dass wir den Gasnotstand managen können"', Capital (website), 1 July 2022, https://www.capital.de/wirtschaft-politik/igbce-chef-vassiliadis--konzerne-wichtiger-als--24-grad-im-wohnzimmer--32502090.html

'Rußland: Neuer Schwung', *Frankfurter Allgemeine Zeitung*, 8 April 2005, https://www.faz.net/aktuell/wirtschaft/russland-neuer-schwung-1234411.html

Jenni Glaser, 'Deindustrialisierung stoppen!', VCI Online, 28 August 2023, https://www.vci.de/services/politikbrief/deindustrialisierung-stoppen-vci-politikbrief.jsp

'Russlands Tor zur Europäischen Union', HamburgInvest, 6 August 2012,

Claus Hecking, 'Trumps Aussagen im Faktencheck: Ist Deutschland ein "Gefangener Russlands"?', *Der Spiegel*, 11 July 2018, https://www.spiegel.de/wirtschaft/soziales/deutschland-ein-gefangener-russlands-donald-trumps-aussagen-im-faktencheck-a-1217900.html

Dirk Holtbrügge, 'Erfahrungen und Perspektiven deutsch-russischer Unternehmenskooperationen', Bayerisch-Russische Fachkonferenz Wirtschaftswissenschaften, Nürnberg, 9 November 2017, https://www.uni-regensburg.de/assets/bayhost/en/laenderinfos/russland-brfk/holtbruegge_key_note_brfk.pdf

Michael Inacker, 'Staatsbesuch in Russland: Unternehmer erleichtern

Merkel die Gespräche', *Handelsblatt*, 16 November 2012, https://www.
handelsblatt.com/meinung/kommentare/staatsbesuch-in-russland-
unternehmer-erleichtern-merkel-die-gespraeche-/7399508.html

Matthias Janson, 'Infografik: Deutschlands Handel mit Russland', Statista
(website), 25 February 2022, https://de.statista.com/infografik/26923/
volumen-des-aussenhandels-zwischen-deutschland-und-russland

Galina Kolev-Schaefer, 'Deutsch-russische Beziehungen', Institut der
deutschen Wirtschaft (IW), 5 February 2015, https://www.iwkoeln.de/
presse/iwd/galina-kolev-deutsch-russische-beziehungen.html

O. König and R. Detje, 'Machtkampf um Gas und Profit', IG Metall
Ennepe-Ruhr-Wupper (website), 8 February 2019, https://www.
sozialismus.de/kommentare_analysen/detail/artikel/machtkampf-um-
gas-und-profit/

Claus-Friedrich Laaser and Klaus Schrader, 'Das deutsche
Russlandgeschäft im Schatten der Krise: Gefährliche Abhängigkeiten?',
Wirtschaftsdienst, 94(5), 2014, pp. 335–43, https://www.wirtschaftsdienst.
eu/inhalt/jahr/2014/heft/5/beitrag/abhaengigkeit-im-deutschen-
russlandgeschaeft.html

Robert Lorenz, 'Gewerkschaftsdämmerung: Geschichte und Perspektiven
deutscher Gewerkschaften', Studien des Göttinger Instituts für
Demokratieforschung zur Geschichte politischer und gesellschaftlicher
Kontroversen, 6, (Bielefeld: transcript Verlag, 2013), https://www.
ssoar.info/ssoar/bitstream/handle/document/70055/ssoar-2013-lorenz-
Gewerkschaftsdammerung_Geschichte_und_Perspektiven_deutscher.
pdf?sequence=1&isAllowed=y&lnkname=ssoar-2013-lorenz-
Gewerkschaftsdammerung_Geschichte_und_Perspektiven_deutscher.
pdf

Dietmar Student and Thomas Werres, 'Zweite Karriere: Die Gerhard-
Schröder-AG', *Manager Magazin*, https://www.manager-magazin.de/
magazin/artikel/a-680306.html

Stefan Meister and Joachim Staron, 'Entfremdete Partner: Deutschland
und Russland', *Osteuropa* 62, no. 6/8, June–August 2012, pp. 475–84,
https://www.jstor.org/stable/44935745.

Bettina Menzel, 'Diese deutschen Unternehmen machen noch immer
dicke Gewinne in Russland', *Frankfurter Rundschau*, 4 July 2023,
https://www.fr.de/wirtschaft/ukraine-krieg-deutschland-unternehmen-
gewinne-russland-92381035.html

Andreas Metz, 'Wirtschaft fordert neue Russland-Strategie', Ost-

Ausschuss der Deutschen Wirtschaft (website), 11 July 2013, https://
www.ost-ausschuss.de/wirtschaft-fordert-neue-russland-strategie

Nette Nöstlinger and Matthew Karnitschnig, 'How Germany Inc. played
Russian roulette – and lost', *Politico*, 13 April 2022, https://www.politico.
eu/article/germany-inc-played-russian-roulette-and-lost-ukraine-war-
energy-gas-trade/

Stefan Reinecke, 'DGB kritisiert Boni-Verbot: Kotau vor den Konzernen',
Tageszeitung, 29 December 2022, https://taz.de/!5897289/

Reuters, 'China und Rußland beflügeln deutschen Außenhandel',
Frankfurter Allgemeine Zeitung, 7 March 2005, https://www.faz.
net/aktuell/wirtschaft/konjunktur/china-und-russland-befluegeln-
deutschen-aussenhandel-1208331.html

Roland Götz, 'Deutschland und Russland – "strategische Partner"?',
Bundeszentrale für politische Bildung (Federal Agency for Civic
Education) (website), 10 March 2006, https://www.bpb.de/shop/
zeitschriften/apuz/29872/deutschland-und-russland-strategische-
partner/

Lukas Paul Schmelter, 'How Germany Lost the Trust of Eastern Europe',
Internationale Politik Quarterly, 4 January 2023, https://ip-quarterly.
com/en/how-germany-lost-trust-eastern-europe

Shannon Schuhmacher and Janell Fetterolf, 'Germany and Merkel Receive
High Marks Internationally in Chancellor's Last Year in Office', Pew
Research Center's Global Attitudes Project, 22 September 2021, https://
www.pewresearch.org/global/2021/09/22/germany-and-merkel-receive-
high-marks-internationally-in-chancellors-last-year-in-office/

Sven C. Singhofen, 'Deutschland und Russland zwischen strategischer
Partnerschaft und neuer Konkurrenz', Konrad Adenauer Stiftung
(website), 22 February 2007, https://www.kas.de/de/arbeitspapiere/
detail/-/content/deutschland-und-russland-zwischen-strategischer-
partnerschaft-und-neuer-konkurrenz1

Klaus Stratmann, 'Industriestrompreis: 400 Mittelständler pochen
ebenfalls auf niedrigeren Strompreis', *Handelsblatt*, 30 August
2023, https://www.handelsblatt.com/politik/deutschland/
industriestrompreis-400-mittelstaendler-pochen-ebenfalls-auf-
niedrigeren-strompreis/29358980.html

'Jörg Schönenborn (WDR) im Gespräch mit Wladimir Putin', Tagesschau
(website), 5 April 2013, https://www.tagesschau.de/multimedia/video/
video-ts-61286.html

Claas Tatje, 'Westenergie-Chefin Riche: "Ob die Anlagen wieder hochgefahren warden, weiß kein Mensch"', *Manager Magazin*, 17 August 2023, https://www.manager-magazin.de/unternehmen/energie/energiewende-wird-die-debatte-ueber-die-energiewende-ehrlich-gefuehrt-frau-reiche-a-b07bf3d8-eb32-4644-9000-02a7de512889?%3Fsara_ecid=nl_upd_vtRmNA6KefdrNuSn5Q7RQq7VZvodaS&nlid=der-tag-manager-magazin-17-30

Justus von Daniels, Annika Joeres and Frederik Richter, 'CORRECTIV verteidigt "Gazprom-Lobby" Recherche gegen Sigmar Gabriel vor Gericht', Correctiv (website), 5 December 2022, https://correctiv.org/aktuelles/russland-ukraine-2/2022/12/05/correctiv-verteidigt-gazprom-lobby-recherche-gegen-sigmar-gabriel-vor-gericht/?lang=de

Guido Westerwelle and Sergej Lawrow, 'Die deutsch-russische Modernisierungspartnerschaft', *Frankfurter Allgemeine Zeitung*, 30 May 2010, https://www.faz.net/aktuell/politik/guido-westerwelle-und-sergej-lawrow-die-deutsch-russische-modernisierungspartnerschaft-1984205.html

CHAPTER 4: THE CHINA SYNDROME

Hendrik Ankenbrand, Henning Peitsmeier, Johannes Pennekamp and Julua Löhr, 'Allianz hinterfragt Olympia-Sponsoring in China', *Frankfurter Allgemeine Zeitung*, 9 December 2021, https://www.faz.net/aktuell/wirtschaft/mehr-wirtschaft/allianz-hinterfragt-olympia-sponsoring-in-china-17675921.html

Richard Baldwin, 'China is the world's sole manufacturing superpower: A line sketch of the rise', VoxEU CEPR (website), 17 January 2024, https://cepr.org/voxeu/columns/china-worlds-sole-manufacturing-superpower-line-sketch-rise

Lucio Baccaro and Erik Neimanns, 'Who wants wage moderation? Trade exposure, export-led growth, and the irrelevance of bargaining structure', *West European Politics*, 45(6), 2022, pp. 1,257–82, https://doi.org/10.1080/01402382.2021.2024010

'Delegationsreisen', Bayerisches Staatsministerium für Wirtschaft, Landesentwicklung und Energie (website), 2 August 2023, https://www.stmwi.bayern.de/wirtschaft/internationalisierung/delegationsreisen/

Maximilian Beer, 'Baerbock verärgert SPD mit China-Politik: "Sollten

Partner nicht öffentlich brüskieren'", *Berliner Zeitung*, 18 April 2023, https://www.berliner-zeitung.de/politik-gesellschaft/annalena-baerbock-veraergert-spd-mit-china-politik-sollten-partner-nicht-oeffentlich-brueskieren-li.338904

Thorsten Benner, 'Cosco will Teil des Hamburger Hafens kaufen: Olaf Scholz darf Chinas Erpressung nicht nachgeben', *Tagesspiegel*, 20 October 2022, https://www.tagesspiegel.de/meinung/soll-cosco-hamburgs-hafen-kaufen-durfen-warum-olaf-scholz-das-auf-keinen-fall-erlauben-sollte-8769544.html

Thorsten Benner, 'China-Reise: Der enthusiastische Handelsreisende Olaf Scholz', *Die Zeit*, 3 November 2022, https://www.zeit.de/politik/deutschland/2022-11/china-reise-olaf-scholz-deutsche-chinapolitik

Frank Bösch, '50 Jahre deutsch-chinesische Beziehungen: Handel durch Wandel', *Frankfurter Allgemeine Zeitung*, 17 October 2022, https://www.faz.net/aktuell/politik/die-gegenwart/50-jahre-deutsch-chinesische-beziehungen-handel-durch-wandel-18391577.html

Lisa Breuer, 'Xinjiang Police Files: Diese deutschen Firmen sind in dem Uiguren-Gebiet Xinjiang aktiv', *Handelsblatt*, 27 May 2022, https://www.handelsblatt.com/politik/xinjiang-police-files-diese-deutschen-firmen-sind-in-dem-uiguren-gebiet-xinjiang-aktiv/28376146.html

M. Brudermüller, R. Busch, B. Garijo, S. Hartung, N. Leibinger-Kammüller, J. Rinnert, K. Rosenfeld and A. Titzrath, 'Dax-Manager zu Globalisierung: Rückzug aus China schneidet uns ab: "Ein Rückzug aus China schneidet uns ab"', *Frankfurter Allgemeine Zeitung*, 10 November 2022, https://www.faz.net/aktuell/wirtschaft/unternehmen/dax-manager-zu-globalisierung-rueckzug-aus-china-schneidet-uns-ab-18448754.html

'Verfassungsschutzbericht 2022', Bundesamt für Verfassungsschutz (website), July 2023, http://www.verfassungsschutz.de/DE/service/publikationen/publikationen_node.html;jsessionid=12A0DAFCE6727B2198CAF68C88F1F00A.intranet662

'Deutschland: Entwicklung des Außenhandels', Bundeszentrale für politische Bildung (website), 13 April 2023, https://www.bpb.de/kurz-knapp/zahlen-und-fakten/globalisierung/52842/deutschland-entwicklung-des-aussenhandels/

'BWA: "China-Strategie" der Bundesregierung nicht im Interesse des deutschen Mittelstands', CRI Online, 15 July 2023, https://german.cri.cn/2023/07/15/ARTIAOkxrr79L0Ch15uswy4r230715.shtml

Susan Christopherson, Jonathan Michie and Peter Tyler, 'Regional resilience: theoretical and empirical perspectives', *Cambridge Journal of Regions, Economy and Society*, 3(1), March 2010, pp. 3–10, https://doi.org/10.1093/cjres/rsq004

Jan Dams, and Anja Ettel, 'Merck-Chefin besorgt über die Langzeitfolgen des Kriegs', *Die Welt*, 2 April 2022, https://www.welt.de/wirtschaft/article237932965/Merck-Chefin-Garijo-Mich-beschaeftigen-die-Langzeitfolgen-dieses-Kriegs-sehr.html

Wolfgang Dauth, Sebastian Findeisen and Jens Südekum, 'The Rise of the East and the Far East: German Labor Markets and Trade Integration', *Journal of the European Economic Association*, 12(6), 1 December 2014, pp. 1,643–75, https://academic.oup.com/jeea/article-abstract/12/6/1643/2319741?redirectedFrom=fulltext&login=false

Frank Dikötter, *China after Mao: The Rise of a Superpower* (London: Bloomsbury, 2022).

Deutsche Presse-Agentur, 'Kretschmann zieht positive Bilanz seiner China-Reise', Die Welt, 24 October 2015, https://www.welt.de/regionales/baden-wuerttemberg/article147991223/Kretschmann-zieht-positive-Bilanz-seiner-China-Reise.html

Deutsche Presse-Agentur, 'Deutsche Industrie hält an »Just in Time« Prinzip fest', *Der Spiegel*, 9 December 2021, https://www.spiegel.de/wirtschaft/deutsche-industrie-haelt-an-just-in-time-fertigung-fest-a-0da16a0c-9313-4e38-9ec3-ec40d14019c3

Deutsche Presse-Agentur, 'Mercedes-Chef hält Entflechtung von China für "Illusion"', Automobilwoche (website), 2 May 2023, https://www.automobilwoche.de/agenturmeldungen/mercedes-chef-ola-kallenius-halt-entflechtung-von-china-fur-illusion

Deutsche Presse-Agentur, 'NRW.Global Business trennt sich von Schröder-Kim', Merkur.de, 16 May 2023, https://www.merkur.de/politik/nrw-global-business-trennt-sich-von-schroeder-kim-zr-92281801.html

Deutsche Presse-Agentur, 'VW verkauft mehr E-Autos als Tesla', *Manager Magazin*, 8 August 2023, https://www.manager-magazin.de/unternehmen/id-modelle-volkswagen-vw-verkauft-mehr-e-autos-als-tesla-a-20bb9dc7-82ad-4bc8-aa54-f03c08c26629

'Abhängigkeit von China doch nicht so groß?', DW (website), 15 February 2023, https://www.dw.com/de/abh%C3%A4ngigkeit-von-china-doch-nicht-so-gro%C3%9F/a-64708594

DW Deutsch, 'Journal Interview: Jürgen Hambrecht', 14 September 2007, YouTube video, https://www.youtube.com/watch?v=sLteGHOPVjY

Thomas Fischer, 'Die Außenbeziehungen der deutschen Länder als Ausdruck "perforierter" nationalstaatlicher Souveränität?', in Hans-Georg Wehling (ed.), *Die Deutschen Länder: Geschichte, Politik, Wirtschaft* (Wiesbaden: VS Verlag für Sozialwissenschaften, 2004), pp. 369–90.

'Bei 5G-Auschluss von Huawei: China droht Deutschland mit Vergeltung', Focus Online, 18 December 2019, https://www.focus.de/finanzen/boerse/aktien/bei-5g-ausschluss-von-huawei-jetzt-droht-china-deutschland-mit-vergeltung_id_11461519.html

'China-Reise von Bundeskanzlerin Merkel vom 28.-30.10.2015 – Teilnehmer der Wirtschaftsdelegation und Bergedorfer Gesprächskreis', FragDenStaat (website), 8 January 2016, https://fragdenstaat.de/anfrage/china-reise-von-bundeskanzlerin-merkel-vom-28-30102015-teilnehmer-der-wirtschaftsdelegation-und-bergedorfer-gesprachskreis/

'Unterlagen zu Lobbykontakten', FragDenStaat (website), 4 January 2023, https://fragdenstaat.de/anfrage/unterlagen-zu-lobbykontakten-7/

Martina Fuchs, 'Risiken weltweiter Wertschöpfungsketten: Maßnahmen und Lernprozesse in deutschen Metallunternehmen nach der Katastrophe in Japan im März 2011', Working Paper, Universität zu Köln, October 2011, https://wigeo.uni-koeln.de/sites/wigeo/Veroeffentlichungen/Working_Paper/WP_2011-01.pdf

Angela Göpfert, 'Was der Teilrückzug Kuwaits für Mercedes-Benz bedeutet: Mercedes und seine ausländischen Aktionäre', Tagesschau (website), 29 March 2023, https://www.tagesschau.de/wirtschaft/finanzen/mercedes-benz-kuwait-china-aktionaere-dividende-101.html

Christian Haegele and Sabrine Schlemmer-Kaune, 'Minister Lies reist mit Wirtschaftsdelegation nach China', Ministerium für Wirtschaft, Verkehr, Bauen und Digitalisierung, 24 May 2017, https://www.mw.niedersachsen.de/startseite/aktuelles/presseinformationen/minister-lies-reist-mit-wirtschaftsdelegation-nach-china-154270.html

Simon Hage, Martin Hesse, Alexander Jung, Peter Müller, Gerald Traufetter and Bernhard Zand, 'Wie abhängig Deutschlands Wirtschaft von China ist', *Der Spiegel*, 24 May 2018, https://www.spiegel.de/spiegel/deutschlands-wirtschaft-ist-von-china-abhaengig-a-1208784.html

'Studie: Deutsche Firmen investieren mehr als je zuvor in China', *Handelsblatt*, 29 March 2023, https://www.handelsblatt.com/politik/international/studie-deutsche-firmen-investieren-mehr-als-je-zuvor-in-china/29067056.html

Jakob Hanke Vela, Giorgio Leali and Barbara Moens, 'Germany's drive for EU–China deal draws criticism from other EU countries', *Politico*, 1 January 2021, https://www.politico.eu/article/germanys-drive-for-eu-china-deal-draws-criticism-from-other-eu-countries/

Dana Heide, 'Interview mit Mikko Huotari: Merics-Chef: "China steht am Wendepunkt"', *Handelsblatt*, 21 July 2023, https://www.handelsblatt.com/politik/international/interview-mit-mikko-huotari-merics-chef-china-steht-am-wendepunkt/29267720.html

Dana Heide, 'Außenhandel: China setzt deutsche Wirtschaft in Europa unter Druck', *Handelsblatt*, 17 August 2023, https://www.handelsblatt.com/politik/international/aussenhandel-china-setzt-deutsche-wirtschaft-in-europa-unter-druck/29330480.html

Christoph Hein, 'Deutscher Konzerne: Machtkampt um die China-Interessen', *Frankfurter Allgemeine Zeitung*, 12 November 2022, https://www.faz.net/aktuell/wirtschaft/china-engagement-deutscher-konzerne-spaltet-die-wirtschaft-18455016.html

Wolfgang Hirn, 'China dreht auf', *Manager Magazin*, 5 November 2004, https://www.manager-magazin.de/magazin/artikel/a-313800.html

Wolfgang Hirn, 'Herausforderung China: Aufbau Ost, Abbau West', *Manager Magazin*, 9 March 2005, https://www.manager-magazin.de/unternehmen/mittelstand/a-344727.html

Wolfgang Hirn, 'Asien-Pazifik-Konferenz der deutschen Wirtschaft: Alternativen zu China – deutsche Unternehmen tun sich schwer', *Manager Magazin*, 5 November 2018, https://www.manager-magazin.de/politik/weltwirtschaft/asien-pazifik-konferenz-der-deutschen-wirtschaft-umgang-mit-china-a-1236730.html

J. Hofer, 'Subventionen für Chiphersteller: "Die 43 Milliarden können nur der Anfang sein"', *Handelsblatt*, 7 August 2023, https://www.handelsblatt.com/technik/it-internet/subventionen-fuer-chiphersteller-die-43-milliarden-koennen-nur-der-anfang-sein/29307324.html

J. Hofer, 'Entscheidung gefallen: TSMC investiert zehn Milliarden Euro in Dresden', *Handelsblatt*, 8 August 2023, https://www.handelsblatt.com/technik/it-internet/entscheidung-gefallen-tsmc-investiert-zehn-milliarden-euro-in-dresden/29313286.html

J. Hofer and J. Olk, 'Halbleiter: Taiwanesischer Chipkonzern TSMC kommt nach Deutschland', *Handelsblatt*, 7 August 2023, https://www. handelsblatt.com/politik/deutschland/halbleiter-taiwanesischer-chipkonzern-tsmc-kommt-nach-deutschland/29306926.html

René Höltschi and Michael Rausch, 'Allianz-Chef Oliver Bäte befürchtet: «Das Schuldenproblem verschiebt sich nach Kerneuropa»', *Neue Zürcher Zeitung*, 25 May 2023, https://www.nzz.ch/wirtschaft/allianz-chef-baete-im-interview-zu-zinswende-und-china-risiken-ld.1737980

Andy Home, 'Europe races to fix its rare earths import dependency', Reuters, 11 October 2021, https://www.reuters.com/business/energy/europe-races-fix-its-rare-earths-import-dependency-andy-home-2021-10-08/

Maren Jensen, ', 'Fliegen ein Kanzler und zwölf Manager nach China', *Manager Magazin*, 3 November 2022, https://www.manager-magazin. de/politik/deutschland/olaf-scholz-reise-nach-peking-diese-12-manager-fliegen-mit-nach-china-a-880f0f38-2d15-4443-8701-df949934beea

Jürgen Matthes, 'Wie ist der starke Importanstieg aus China im Jahr 2022 zu erklären und wie haben sich die Import-Abhängigkeiten entwickelt?', *IW-Report*, no. 34, 20 June 2023, https://www.iwkoeln.de/studien/juergen-matthes-wie-ist-der-starke-importanstieg-aus-china-im-jahr-2022-zu-erklaeren-und-wie-haben-sich-die-import-abhaengigkeiten-entwickelt. html

Katrin Kamin and Rolf Langhammer, 'Gastkommentar: Die deutsche China-Strategie zeigt richtige Ansätze, bleibt aber unkonkret in ihren Instrumenten', *Handelsblatt*, 27 July 2023, https://www.handelsblatt. com/meinung/gastbeitraege/gastkommentar-die-deutsche-china-strategie-zeigt-richtige-ansaetze-bleibt-aber-unkonkret-in-ihren-instrumenten/29272202.html

Heiner Kiesel, 'Das "Just-in-Time"-Prinzip: Alles muss fließen', Deutschlandfunk Kultur (website), 13 October 2020, https://www. deutschlandfunkkultur.de/das-just-in-time-prinzip-alles-muss-fliessen-100.html

Ruth Kirchner, 'IW-Studie: Abhängigkeit von China so groß wie nie', Tagesschau (website), 10 February 2023, https://www.tagesschau.de/ wirtschaft/weltwirtschaft/china-handel-abhaengigkeit-101.html

Claus-Peter Köth, 'Automobilindustrie begrüßt den Deal', *Automobil Industrie*, 31 December 2020, https://www.automobil-industrie.vogel. de/automobilindustrie-begruesst-den-deal-a-989268/

Riccardo Kurto, 'Rückzug aus China für viele Unternehmen "kein Thema"', BME (website), 14 March 2023, https://www.bme.de/news/rueckzug-aus-china-fuer-viele-unternehmen-kein-thema

Kai Küstner, 'Klartext, Bekenntnisse und eine Zauberformel', Tagesschau (website), 15 July 2023, https://www.tagesschau.de/inland/innenpolitik/china-strategie-bundesregierung-100.html

Andreas Macho, '"Totalverlust"? Die China-Wette von BASF wird immer riskanter', *Die Welt*, 28 April 2023, https://www.welt.de/wirtschaft/article245016430/BASF-Totalverlust-Die-China-Wette-wird-immer-riskanter.html

Markus Demary and Michael Grömling, 'Aussagekraft der Auftragseingänge der deutschen Industrie', *IW-Trends*, no. 3, 31 July 2011, https://www.iwkoeln.de/studien/markus-demary-michael-groemling-aussagekraft-der-auftragseingaenge-der-deutschen-industrie-53439.html

Jürgen Matthes, 'Vorsicht beim Abkommen mit China', Institut der deutschen Wirtschaft (IW), 16 June 2023, https://www.iwkoeln.de/presse/in-den-medien/juergen-matthes-vorsicht-beim-abkommen-mit-china.html

Sebastian Matthes, 'Interview: Siemens-Chef Busch warnt: "Nicht zum Spielball zwischen USA und China warden"', *Handelblatt*, 9 November 2021, https://www.handelsblatt.com/unternehmen/management/interview-siemens-chef-busch-warnt-nicht-zum-spielball-zwischen-usa-und-china-werden/27771254.html

Sebastian Matthes and Theresa Rauffmann, 'Interview: Merck-Chefin hält Abkoppelung von China "in den nächsten zwei Jahrzehnten für nicht machbar"', *Handelsblatt*, 4 July 2023, https://www.handelsblatt.com/unternehmen/industrie/interview-merck-chefin-haelt-abkoppelung-von-china-in-den-naechsten-zwei-jahrzehnten-fuer-nicht-machbar/29231640.html

Anja Müller, 'Chinageschäft: Mittelstand steuert bei Lieferketten um – Abhängigkeit von China bleibt aber hoch', *Handelsblatt*, 5 December 2022, https://www.handelsblatt.com/unternehmen/mittelstand/chinageschaeft-mittelstand-steuert-bei-lieferketten-um-abhaengigkeit-von-china-bleibt-aber-hoch/28845598.html

Jens Münchrath, 'Clemens Fuest im Interview: "Es kann sinnvoll sein, deutsche Großunternehmen zu zerschlagen"', *Handelsblatt*, 11 February 2019, https://www.handelsblatt.com/politik/deutschland/

clemens-fuest-im-interview-es-kann-sinnvoll-sein-deutsche-grossunternehmen-zu-zerschlagen/23972870.html

Vincent Ni, 'EU parliament "freezes" China trade deal over sanctions', *The Guardian*, 20 May 2021, https://www.theguardian.com/world/2021/may/20/eu-parliament-freezes-china-trade-deal-over-sanctions

'NRW goes to China – Unternehmerreise ins Reich der Mitte', Kooperation International (website), NRW International, 31 March 2010, https://www.kooperation-international.de/aktuelles/nachrichten/detail/info/nrw-goes-to-china-unternehmerreise-ins-reich-der-mitte/

'Nokia macht in Rumänien dicht', NTV (website), 29 September 2011, https://www.n-tv.de/wirtschaft/Nokia-macht-in-Rumaenien-dicht-article4416656.html

Niklas Ottersbach, 'Zukunftsinvestitionen gegen Staatsknete', 27 June 2023, Deutschlandfunk (website), https://www.deutschlandfunk.de/intel-fabrik-chips-subventionen-magdeburg-100.html

Jan Pasemann and Martin Bork, 'Kosten sparen in der Krise: Der Gang ins Ausland sichert auch den heimischen Standort', PwC (website), 7 December 2011, https://www.pwc.de/de/internationale-maerkte/kosten-sparen-in-der-krise.html

'Commission launches investigation on subsidised electric cars from China', European Commission, press release, 4 October 2023, https://ec.europa.eu/commission/presscorner/detail/en/ip_23_4752

'Experte sieht Chancen für Wirtschaftsraum mit Russland', Produktion (website), 6 April 2021, https://www.produktion.de/wirtschaft/experte-sieht-chancen-fuer-wirtschaftsraum-mit-russland-374.html

'PV-Anlagen: Fast 90 Prozent kommen aus China', LeadersNet Deutschland (website), 1 March 2023, https://www.leadersnet.de/news/67195,pv-anlagen-fast-90-prozent-kommen-aus-china.html

Theresa Rauffmann, 'Chemiekonzern: BASF will nach Gewinneinbruch Milliarden sparen', *Handelsblatt*, 29 July 2023, https://www.handelsblatt.com/unternehmen/industrie/chemiekonzern-basf-will-nach-gewinneinbruch-milliarden-sparen/29284178.html

J. Rudnicka, 'Chinas Anteil am Außenhandel von Deutschland bis 2022', Statista (website), 19 April 2023, https://de.statista.com/statistik/daten/studie/1287627/umfrage/chinas-anteil-am-aussenhandel-von-deutschland/

J. Rudnicka, 'Deutsche Exporte nach China bis 2022', Statista (website), 24 June 2024, https://de.statista.com/statistik/daten/studie/152360/umfrage/deutsche-exporte-nach-china/

A. Sandkamp, V. Stamer, F. Wendorff and S. Gans, 'Leere Regale made in China: Wenn China beim Handel mauert', *Kiel Policy Brief*, 164, 2023, https://www.ifw-kiel.de/de/publikationen/kiel-policy-briefs/2023/leere-regale-made-in-china-wenn-china-beim-handel-mauert-0/

'Germany's China City no more: how failed plans for Duisburg reflect Europe's changing view of Beijing', *South China Morning Post*, 1 July 2023, https://www.scmp.com/magazines/post-magazine/long-reads/article/3225919/germanys-china-city-no-more-how-failed-plans-duisburg-reflect-europes-changing-view-beijing

Arne Semsrott, 'Guttenbergs kurzer Draht zu Merkel: So hofierte das Kanzleramt Wirecard', FragDenStaat (website), 9 October 2020, https://fragdenstaat.de/blog/2020/10/09/wirecard-merkel-guttenberg-china-lobbyismus/

Stefan Stahl, 'Interview: Früherer SPD-Chef Scharping: Man darf China nicht an die Wand nageln', *Augsburger Allgemeine*, 21 January 2022, https://www.augsburger-allgemeine.de/politik/exklusiv-fruecherer-spd-chef-scharping-man-darf-china-nicht-an-die-wand-nageln-id61545316.html

A. Stolte, 'Beschaffungslogistik im China-Geschäft: Kosten—Prozesse—Strategien; Eine Studie von PricewaterhouseCoopers in Zusammenarbeit mit dem Bundesverband Materialwirtschaft, Einkauf und Logistik e. V.', PwC) 2008, https://docplayer.org/70272923-Beschaffungslogistik-im-china-geschaeft-kosten-prozesse-strategien-herausgegeben-von-pricewaterhousecoopers.html

'BASF-Chef beklagt "China-Bashing"', Tagesschau (website), 26 October 2022, https://www.tagesschau.de/wirtschaft/basf-chef-brudermueller-china-bashing-wegkommen-101.html

'Top-Ökonomen kritisieren Intel-Subvention scharf', Tagesschau (website), 19 June 2023, https://www.tagesschau.de/wirtschaft/unternehmen/intel-foederung-subvention-kritik-oekonomen-100.html

'China – Delegationsreise der Bundesregierung mit guten Ergebnissen', Verband der Fleischwirtschaft, 4 September 2012, https://www.v-d-f.de/news/pm-20120904-0209

Claudia von Salzen and Cornelius Dieckmann, 'Reisen nach Peking und ein geheimer Verein: Wie deutsche Politiker sich für Chinas Regime starkmachen', *Tagesspiegel*, 16 June 2023, https://www.tagesspiegel.de/politik/reisen-nach-peking-und-ein-geheimer-verein-wie-deutsche-politiker-sich-fur-chinas-regime-starkmachen-9989776.html

Martin Wambach, *Unternehmerische Erwartung trifft ausländische Realität ⊠ Bestandsaufnahme, Erfahrungen und Empfehlungen zur Steuerung von Auslandsgesellschaften* (Cologne: Rödl & Partner, 2018), https://www.roedl.de/de-de/de/medien/publikationen/buecher/international/documents/unternehmerische-erwartung-roedl-partner.pdf

Stefan Weinzierl, 'Entkopplung? China bremst Shoppingtour in Europa', 21 February 2023, Produktion (website), https://www.produktion.de/wirtschaft/entkopplung-china-bremst-shoppingtour-in-europa-662.html

Horst Wildemann, 'Just-in-Time-Lösungskonzepte in Deutschland', *Manager Magazin*, 7 January 1986, https://www.manager-magazin.de/harvard/just-in-time-loesungskonzepte-in-deutschland-a-ecb9f181-0002-0001-0000-000029861778

'Trade (% of GDP)—Date for Germany, China, United Kingdom, United States', World Bank Open Data, 2023, https://prosperitydata360.worldbank.org/en/indicator/WB+WDI+NE+TRD+GNFS+ZS

Y. Yang and P. Nilsson, 'Volkswagen, BMW and Mercedes hit by Xinjiang forced labour complaint', *Financial Times*, 20 June 2023, https://www.ft.com/content/688470e9-d335-4c85-83d3-67ea64891035

'Johnson: Ampel wollte vor Kriegsbeginn ukrainische Aufgabe', ZDF (website), 23 November 2022, https://www.zdf.de/uri/od3d56f1-3c55-493d-8c67-c28bf603d501

'Bayern ist Importland', *Süddeutsche Zeitung*, 19 June 2022, https://www.sueddeutsche.de/bayern/import-export-aussenhandelsdefizit-bayern-wirtschaft-1.5605087

CHAPTER 5: BREAKING THE BREAK

Peter Bofinger, and Gustav Horn, 'Die Schuldenbremse gefährdet die gesamtwirtschaftliche Stabilität und die Zukunft unserer Kinder', n.d., retrieved 18 April 2024, https://www.boeckler.de/pdf/imk_appell_schuldenbremse.pdf

Gordon Brown, Budget Statement (London: Hansard, 2 July 1997), https://api.parliament.uk/historic-hansard/commons/1997/jul/02/budget-statement

'Zweites Nachtragshaushaltsgesetz 2021 ist nichtig', Bundesverfassungsgericht, press release, 15 November 2023, https://

www.bundesverfassungsgericht.de/SharedDocs/Pressemitteilungen/
DE/2023/bvg23-101.html

'Daily Newsbriefing', Eurointelligence (website), 5 November 2008,
https://www.eurointelligence.com (subscription only)

'Daily Newsbriefing', Eurointelligence (website), 22 April 2009, https://
www.eurointelligence.com (subscription only)

Michael Hüther and Jens Südekum, 'How to re-design German fiscal
policy rules after the COVID19 pandemic: Study commissioned by
Forum New Economy', Forum New Economy Working Papers, no. 2,
Berlin, 17 November 2020, https://www.iwkoeln.de/studien/michael-
huether-jens-suedekum-how-to-re-design-german-fiscal-policy-rules-
after-the-covid19-pandemic.html

Wolfgang Münchau, 'Berlin weaves a deficit hair-shirt for us all', *Financial
Times*, 21 June 2009, https://www.ft.com/content/4e63cb22-5e8b-11de-
91ad-00144feabdc0

S. Schmid, 'Bundestag stimmt für Schuldenbremse im Grundgesetz',
Deutscher Bundestag (website), 2020, https://webarchiv.bundestag.
de/archive/2010/0427/dokumente/textarchiv/2009/24572764_kw22_
foedkom_sp/index.html

'Haushaltsdefizit: Blauer Brief für Hans Eichel', *Der Spiegel*, 29 January
2002, https://www.spiegel.de/wirtschaft/haushaltsdefizit-blauer-brief-
fuer-hans-eichel-a-179631.html

CHAPTER 6: WE AND THE OTHERS

Agence France-Presse, 'Fachkräftemangel: Gewerkschaften warnen
vor »Personalkollaps« im öffentlichen Dienst', *Der Spiegel*, 8 August
2023, https://www.spiegel.de/wirtschaft/fachkraeftemangel-
gewerkschaften-warnen-vor-personalkollaps-im-oeffentlichen-dienst-
a-5e9b4775-5763-4196-86f6-9494fac7e664

Mohamed Amjahid, 'Deutschland für Fachkräfte unattraktiv: "Oh, wow"',
Tageszeitung, 11 March 2023, https://taz.de/!5918453/

Werner Beutnagel, 'Fachkräftemangel erreicht Rekordniveau',
Automobil Produktion (website), 2 August 2022, https://www.
automobil-produktion.de/management/fachkraeftemangel-erreicht-
rekordniveau-111.html

Benjamin Bidder, 'Ostdeutsche Wirtschaft: Wo Rassismus zum

Standortrisiko wird', *Der Spiegel*, 3 July 2023, https://www.spiegel.de/wirtschaft/soziales/wirtschaft-und-die-afd-wie-fremdenhass-zum-standortrisiko-wird-a-4e0d58cc-625f-4c88-acd2-7983e2b5b866

Ulrike Bosse, 'Gekommen – und geblieben: Die "Gastarbeiter"', NDR (website), 2 March 2022, https://www.ndr.de/geschichte/chronologie/Gastarbeiter-in-Deutschland-Gekommen-und-geblieben,gastarbeiter258.html

Aimie Bouju, 'Die parlamentarische Repräsentation von Menschen mit Migrationsgeschichte im Bundestag', Bundeszentrale für politische Bildung (website), 28 November 2022, https://www.bpb.de/themen/migration-integration/kurzdossiers/514281/die-parlamentarische-repraesentation-von-menschen-mit-migrationsgeschichte-im-bundestag/

'Bevölkerung mit Migrationshintergrund', Bundeszentrale für politische Bildung (website), 24 April 2024, https://www.bpb.de/kurz-knapp/zahlen-und-fakten/soziale-situation-in-deutschland/61646/bevoelkerung-mit-migrationshintergrund/

Elif Can, Clara Milena Konrad, Sidra Khan-Gökkaya, Isabel Molwitz, Jawed Nawabi, Jin Yamamura, Bernd Hamm and Sarah Keller, 'Foreign Healthcare Professionals in Germany: A Questionnaire Survey Evaluating Discrimination Experiences and Equal Treatment at Two Large University Hospitals' *Healthcare* 2002, 10(12), 2339, https://doi.org/10.3390/healthcare10122339

Sophie Crocoll, 'Fachkräftemangel: Warum Hochqualifizierte Deutschland den Rücken kehren', *WirtschaftsWoche*, 24 August 2021, https://www.wiwo.de/politik/deutschland/fachkraeftemangel-warum-hochqualifizierte-deutschland-den-ruecken-kehren/27545944.html

I. Daniel and Reuters, 'DIHK-Umfrage: Jedes zweite Unternehmen kann nicht alle Lehrstellen besetzen', *Die Zeit*, 23 August 2023, https://www.zeit.de/arbeit/2023-08/dihk-umfrage-ausbildungsstellen-unbesetzt-haelfte-betriebe

'Neues Staatsbürgerschaftsrecht in Kraft getreten', Deutschlandfunk (website), 19 April 2019, https://www.deutschlandfunk.de/staatsbuergerschaftsrecht-wie-die-regierung-einbuergerung-erleichtern-will-102.html

Florian Diekmann, 'Fachkräftemangel: Seid umschlungen, Millionen!' *Der Spiegel*, 4 July 2023, https://www.spiegel.de/wirtschaft/fachkraeftemangel-und-zuwanderung-seid-umschlungen-millionen-a-212b47b9-7610-4bcd-8675-d54cab9c12cd

Florian Diekmann, 'Mismatch am Jobmarkt: Fachkräfte dringend gesucht, Hilfsarbeiter im Überfluss', *Der Spiegel*, 14 July 2023, https://www. spiegel.de/wirtschaft/arbeitsmarkt-fachkraefte-dringend-gesucht-hilfsarbeiter-im-ueberfluss-a-381b139d-cf6c-417e-b245-5b61bf9e0639

Inga Diercks, 'Job Application in Germany—The Photo Issue', Bucerius Law School (website), 2 September 2019, https://www.law-school.de/ international/article/job-application-in-germany-the-photo-issue

Deutsche Presse-Agentur, 'Die Elite ist weiß und kommt aus dem Westen: Ostdeutsche und Nachfahren von Migranten in Spitzenjobs unterrepräsentiert', *Tagesspiegel*, 26 October 2020, https://www. tagesspiegel.de/politik/ostdeutsche-und-nachfahren-von-migranten-in-spitzenjobs-unterreprasentiert-4157497.html

Deutsche Presse-Agentur, 'Großteil der hochqualifizierten Einwanderer bleibt längerfristig', *Der Spiegel*, 21 July 2023, https://www.spiegel.de/ wirtschaft/deutschland-grossteil-der-hochqualifizierten-einwanderer-bleibt-laengerfristig-a-49b33f75-071d-4939-89e7-6c37e4f0dc3e

Deutsche Presse-Agentur, '"Desaströse Familienpolitik": AfD-Chef will dem Fachkräftemangel mit mehr deutschem Nachwuchs begegnen', *Tagesspiegel*, 6 August 2023, https://www.tagesspiegel. de/politik/desastrose-familienpolitik-afd-chef-chrupalla-will-dem-fachkraftemangel-mit-mehr-deutschem-nachwuchs-begegnen-10270558.html

Deutsche Presse-Agentur, 'Streit um Einbürgerungsreform: CDU-Chef Merz warnt vor "Einwanderung in Sozialsysteme"', t-online (website), 28 November 2022, https://www.t-online.de/-/100087958

'Fachkräfteeinwanderungsgesetz: Neue Wege zur Fachkräftegewinnung', Bundesregierung (website), 23 May 2024, https://www. bundesregierung.de/breg-de/themen/arbeit-und-soziales/ fachkraefteeinwanderungsgesetz-2182168

'Integration: Schlechtere Bewerbungschancen mit ausländischen Namen', *Frankfurter Allgemeine Zeitung*, 26 March 2014, https://www.faz.net/ aktuell/politik/inland/integration-auslaendische-vornamen-mindern-bewerbungschancen-12865379.html

Martin Ganslmeier, 'Kommentar: Modernes Staatsbürgerschaftsrecht ist richtig', Tagesschau (website), 29 November 2022, https://www. tagesschau.de/kommentar/staatsbuergerrecht-101.html

Government of Canada, 2022 Annual Report to Parliament on Immigration, Government of Canada (website), 1 November 2022, https://www.

canada.ca/en/immigration-refugees-citizenship/corporate/publications-manuals/annual-report-parliament-immigration-2022.html

Janne Grote and Paula Hoffmeyer-Zlotnik, 'Anwerbung und Bindung von internationalen Studierenden', BAMF – Bundesamt für Migration und Flüchtlinge (website), 11 March 2019, https://www.BAMF.de/SharedDocs/Anlagen/DE/EMN/Studien/wp85-internationale-studierende.html?nn=282022

David Gutensohn, 'Fachkräftemangel: "Deutschland strahlt vor allem Bürokratie aus"', *Die Zeit*, 14 March 2023, https://www.zeit.de/arbeit/2023-02/fachkraeftemangel-ausland-einwanderung-gesetz-institut-der-zukunft-der-arbeit/komplettansicht

Rieke Havertz, 'Hubertus Heil und Annalena Baerbock: Ein brasilianischer Pflegetraum', *Die Zeit*, 5 June 2023, https://www.zeit.de/politik/ausland/2023-06/hubertus-heil-brasilien-fachkraeftemangel/komplettansicht

K. Heflik and Deutsche Presse-Agentur, Bundesagentur für Arbeit: Löhne in Berufen mit Fachkräftemangel oft unterdurchschnittlich', *Die Zeit*, 24 February 2020, https://www.zeit.de/arbeit/2020-02/fachkraefte-einkommen-bundesagentur-fuer-arbeit

Hoffmeyer-Zlotnik, P., & Grote, J. (n.d.). *Anwerbung und Bindung von internationalen Studierenden in Deutschland.*

Kemal Hür, '60 Jahre Gastarbeiter in Deutschland: "Ich habe mir immer gewünscht, dass ich nach Deutschland komme"', Deutschlandfunk (website), 7 December 2015, https://www.deutschlandfunk.de/60-jahre-gastarbeiter-in-deutschland-ich-habe-mir-immer-100.html

B. Hyun, 'Geheime Rüstungsgeschäfte mit Russland? Rheinmetall äußert sich', *Merkur.de (website)*, 2 August 2023, https://www.merkur.de/politik/putin-recherche-ukraine-krieg-rheinmetall-ruestungsgeschaefte-waffen-92433475.html

Katharina James, 'Lehrlingsmangel: Fast 40.000 Ausbildungsplätze in Handwerksbetrieben sind unbesetzt', *Die Zeit*, 18 May 2023, https://www.zeit.de/wirtschaft/2023-05/ausbildungsplaetze-lehrlingsmangel-handwerksbetriebe

Katharina James and Agence France-Presse, 'Staatsbürgerschaft: Union und FDP kritisieren geplante Änderung des Einbürgerungsrechts', *Die Zeit*, 28 November 2022, https://www.zeit.de/politik/deutschland/2022-11/staatsbuergerschaft-aenderung-kritik-union-fdp

Katharina James and Deutsche Presse-Agentur, 'Bildung: Lehrerverband

fordert Migrationsquoten an Schulen', *Die Zeit*, 5 January 2023, https://
www.zeit.de/politik/deutschland/2023-01/lehrerverband-heinz-peter-
meidinger-schulen-migrationsquoten

Claire Jones, 'Why German wages need to rise – and fast', *Financial Times*,
16 November 2016, https://www.ft.com/content/a7758d5e-8566-11e6-
8897-2359a58ac7a5

Julica Jungehülsing and Agence France-Presse, 'AfD: Wirtschaftsweise
fürchtet Abschreckung ausländischer Fachkräfte', *Die Zeit*, 15 July 2023,
https://www.zeit.de/politik/deutschland/2023-07/wirtschaftsweise-
ulrike-malmendier-afd-abschottung-wirtschaftsstandort

Florian Kistler, 'Ausländische Fachkräfte: Ein kleines deutsches
Einwanderungswunder', *WirtschaftsWoche*, 25 August 2023, https://www.
wiwo.de/politik/deutschland/auslaendische-fachkraefte-ein-kleines-
deutsches-einwanderungswunder/29352616.html

Ben Knight, 'Schreckt der Erfolg der AfD ausländische Fachkräfte ab?',
DW (website), 8 July 2023, https://www.dw.com/de/schreckt-der-
erfolg-der-afd-ausl%C3%A4ndische-fachkr%C3%A4fte-ab/a-66155091

Orkan Kösemen, 'Policy Brief Migration: Willkommenskultur in
Deutschland', Bertelsmann Stiftung, 4 Decembr 2017, https://www.
bertelsmann-stiftung.de/de/publikationen/publikation/did/policy-
brief-migration-willkommenskultur-in-deutschland

M. McAuliffe and A. Triandafyllidou, *World Migration Report 2022*
(Geneva: International Organization for Migration, 2021), https://
publications.iom.int/books/world-migration-report-2022

Milena Merten, 'Arbeitsmarkt: Wie Vorurteile den Fachkräftemangel
verstärkt', *Handelsblatt*, 22 August 2023, https://www.handelsblatt.com/
karriere/arbeitsmarkt-wie-schubladendenken-den-fachkraeftemangel-
verstaerkt-/29336740.html

Steven Micksch, 'Frankfurt: "Ausländerbehörde ist Ort des Schreckens"',
Frankfurter Rundschau, 19 January 2023, https://www.fr.de/frankfurt/
des-schreckens-frankfurt-auslaenderbehoerde-ist-ort-92031501.html

Nic Mitchell, 'Universities compete by teaching in English', BBC
News (website), 3 February 2016, https://www.bbc.com/news/
business-35429233

Hans Monath, 'Kritik am Ampel-Plan: Union stellt sich gegen leichtere
Einbürgerung', *Tagesspiegel*, 27 November 2022, https://www.
tagesspiegel.de/politik/kritik-am-ampel-plan-union-stellt-sich-gegen-
leichtere-einburgerung-8926342.html

J. Moreno, 'Wieso wurdest du als Kind so hart bestraft, Fatih Çevikollu?', *Moreno+1* (podcast), *Der Spiegel*, 22 August 2023, https://omny.fm/shows/juan-moreno-plus1-interview-podcast/wieso-hat-dein-vater-dich-verpr-gelt-fatih-evikoll

Dietmar Neuerer and Frank Specht, 'Arbeitskräfte: Wie deutsche Bürokratie die Einwanderung von Fachkräften erschwert', *Handelsblatt*, 21 March 2023, https://www.handelsblatt.com/politik/deutschland/arbeitskraefte-wie-deutsche-buerokratie-die-einwanderung-von-fachkraeften-erschwert/29049460.html

Martin Nóe and Michael Freitag, '"Siggi" wollte Conti-Fabrik in Russland zum Schnäppchenpreis', *Manager Magazin*, 20 March 2023, https://www.manager-magazin.de/unternehmen/autoindustrie/continental-und-volkswagen-wie-siggi-wolf-in-kaluga-ein-automobilkombinat-aufbauen-wollte-a-c6007db5-630f-4882-8ff2-fbed9f6e89de

OECD, *Recruiting Immigrant Workers: Germany 2013* (Paris: OECD, 2013), https://doi.org/10.1787/9789264189034-en

Jonathan Packroff, 'German wage restraint could endanger eurozone stability', Euractiv (website), 3 November 2022, https://www.euractiv.com/section/economy-jobs/news/german-wage-restraint-could-endanger-eurozone-stability/

R. Pascoe, 'English takes over at Dutch universities, just 40% of courses still in Dutch', DutchNews (website), 26 August 2016, https://www.dutchnews.nl/2016/08/english-takes-over-at-dutch-universities-just-40-of-courses-still-in-dutch/

Mathias Peer and Agence France-Presse, Fachkräftemangel: Bundesregierung verhandelt mit sechs Staaten über Migrationsabkommen', *Die Zeit*, 9 August 2023, https://www.zeit.de/politik/deutschland/2023-08/fachkraeftemangel-migrationsabkommen-verhandlungen-bundesregierung

Benedikt Peters, 'Studie: Diskriminierung nach Herkunft bei der Bewerbung; Arbeitsmarkt: Passt nicht zu uns', *Süddeutsche Zeitung*, 7 December 2022, https://www.sueddeutsche.de/politik/bewerbung-diskriminierung-auslaender-1.5711270

Uta Rasche, 'Ausländer in Deutschland: Einwanderungsland wider Willen', *Frankfurter Allgemeine Zeitung*, 11 October 2010, https://www.faz.net/aktuell/feuilleton/sarrazin/analyse-deutschland-ein-einwanderungsland-wider-willen-1580276.html

Doreen Reinhard, 'AfD in Ostdeutschland: "Es wäre naiv zu denken, wir hätten keine AfD-Anhänger in der Firma"', *Die Zeit*, 26 July 2023, https://www.zeit.de/wirtschaft/2023-07/afd-wahlerfolge-ostdeutschland-ddr-wiedervereinigung/komplettansicht

Reuters, 'Hohe Hürden: Fachkräfte sehen Willkommenskultur nach Umzug kritischer', *Tagesspiegel*, 7 July 2023, https://www.tagesspiegel.de/wirtschaft/hohe-hurden-fachkrafte-sehen-willkommenskultur-nach-umzug-kritischer-10111792.html

Annabelle Seubert and Anne Ackermann, 'Ausländerbehörde: "Der schlimmste Ort aller Zeiten"', *Die Zeit*, 4 June 2023, https://www.zeit.de/gesellschaft/2023-05/darmstadt-auslaenderbehoerde-amt-untaetigkeit/komplettansicht

Vera Sprothen, 'Fachkräftemangel: Handwerk und Bauwirtschaft kritisieren geplantes Einwanderungsgesetz', *Die Zeit*, 27 April 2023, https://www.zeit.de/wirtschaft/2023-04/fachkraeftemangel-einwanderung-gesetz-verbaende-kritik

Statista Research Department, 'Anzahl der internationalen Studierenden an Hochschulen in Deutschland im Wintersemester 2022/2023 nach Herkunftsländern', Statista (website), August 2023, https://de.statista.com/statistik/daten/studie/301225/umfrage/auslaendische-studierende-in-deutschland-nach-herkunftslaendern/

'Studienjahr 2022: 10 % mehr ausländische Studienanfängerinnen und -anfänger', Statistisches Bundesamt, press release, 10 March 2023, https://www.destatis.de/DE/Presse/Pressemitteilungen/2023/03/PD23_097_213.html

'Ein Drittel der internationalen Studierenden bleibt langfristig in Deutschland', Statistisches Bundesamt, press release, 12 October 2022, https://www.destatis.de/DE/Presse/Pressemitteilungen/2022/10/PD22_435_12.html

Verena Töpper, 'Letzter Platz: Deutschland', *Manager Magazin*, 21 March 2023, https://www.manager-magazin.de/karriere/internations-umfrage-was-expats-von-deutschland-halten-a-95dd9f23-1c18-4264-876a-11a2c70e454d

Verena Töpper, '„Die Leute hier sind mir zu unterkühlt, direkt und unfreundlich"', *Manager Magazin*, 11 July 2023, https://www.manager-magazin.de/unternehmen/expats-warum-deutschland-auslaendische-fachkraefte-ungluecklich-macht-a-bbb1b539-fb84-4538-a615-e7af42371e76

Verena Töpper, 'Sie wollten zurück nach Deutschland, nun bleiben

sie lieber in Oxford', *Der Spiegel*, 19 August 2023, https://www.
spiegel.de/karriere/fachkraeftemangel-in-deutschland-auswanderer-
berichten-warum-sie-nicht-heimkehren-a-366e2164-0a41-42b2-96f0-
dc22d5ea23b8

Sarah Vojta and Deutsche Presse-Agentur, 'Heinz-Peter Meidinger:
Lehrerpräsident gegen Englischunterricht an allen Grundschulen', *Die
Zeit*, 9 June 2023, https://www.zeit.de/gesellschaft/schule/2023-06/
deutscher-lehrerverband-heinz-peter-meidinger-englischunterricht

Vanessa Vu and Philip Faigle, 'Geflüchtete am Arbeitsmarkt: "Jeder,
der arbeitet, hilft"', *Die Zeit*, 27 July 2023, https://www.zeit.de/
wirtschaft/2023-07/gefluechtete-arbeitsmarkt-integration-boris-
palmer-ruud-koopmans-iab

Vanessa Vu and Nikita Teryoshin, 'Migranten: Sie werden die Mächtigen
sein', *Die Zeit*, 30 May 2023, https://www.zeit.de/gesellschaft/2023-05/
migration-gesellschaft-einwanderung-deutschland-demografischer-
wandel/komplettansicht

Index

KAPUT

KAPUT

INDEX

KAPUT

KAPUT